The Struggle Within

RACE RELATIONS

THE
STRUGGLE
WITHIN

IN THE UNITED STATES

By David Bowen

A W. W. NORTON BOOK
Published by
GROSSET & DUNLAP
A National General Company
New York

CONTENTS

ACKNOWLEDGMENTS

The material in these pages was gathered from the files of newspapers and magazines, from racist pamphlets and the Congressional Record, from books both old and new. Most important of all, it has come from conversations with all kinds of people. All quoted words that are not identified by name were actually spoken in conversations or in public meetings.

The quotation on page 38 is from a collection of reminiscences by former slaves, edited by B. A. Botkin under the title *Lay My Burden Down* (University of Chicago Press). The story at the beginning of Chapter 7 happened to Calvin Kytle, who wrote about it in the *Saturday Review* of May 30, 1964 under the title "Testament of a Transplanted White Southerner." It is retold here with permission. The quotation from Lillian Smith on page 99 is from her book *Killers of the Dream* (W. W. Norton).

The revision owes a great deal to the twenty-eight students—black, white and *chicano*—who undertook to explore with me "The Negro Experience in America" in a course offered at St. Mary's University in the fall of 1970.

David Bowen
San Antonio, Texas
July 31, 1971

PREFACE

No BOOK on this subject can pretend to be absolutely fair, giving the same weight to all the arguments about segregation, integration and the equality or inequality of races. I have tried, but there is no way to think about these questions honestly without coming away with some deep feelings. Those feelings will certainly show through in the following pages.

What this book does try to do is to take all the arguments seriously. This means bringing into the open many questions that lie under the surface of the debate over race relations and civil rights.

How do white people look at black people? Why do they see them in this way? What do Negroes think of whites, and of themselves? *Are* Negroes "different" from other people? If so, in what ways? How important are these differences?

How do some people—even some Negroes—profit from racial discrimination? How do American ideas about Negroes fit in with American ideas about equality? Is it possible to change the way we behave toward people of other races? Whose job is this: the schools', the churches', the law's? Why does the black American need special attention anyway?

Some people will not think it polite to raise questions like these. But these questions lie beneath all the arguments about civil rights for nonwhites. There is no point pretending they do not exist. If this book succeeds in nothing else, it ought to show that such questions are not as simple as we may have thought them before.

For one thing, things don't stay the same. There is no point talking about *the* civil rights movement. The movement has been going on for 200 years and it has taken many forms. No "snapshot" of it, taken at one time and place, can tell much about it. Only a "moving picture" can make it clear how the movement grows and changes, how it speaks with many voices, not all saying the same thing.

In the few years since this book first appeared (in 1965), the struggle has changed basically. That was a year of great optimism. Two monumental civil rights acts made it easy to believe that the American Negro had finally secured the rights promised him at the close of the Civil War. "Integration" was the key word. But of course it was not that easy; the problems were too deep.

Under the pressure of the war in Southeast Asia, young people both black and white began to re-examine American society. A good many Negroes doubt now whether integration into this society makes sense, even if it could be done. They talk of "separation," "power," "black nationalism." Many more are still trying to find a way to bring black and white together in one society. But few, very few, still care about simply bringing blacks into an unchanged white society.

It is not too much to say that since 1965 only two things have *not* changed: the Negro's demand to be recognized as a human being and a citizen, and the white's basic fear of what would happen if this really came about.

A Negro scholar named W. E. B. DuBois predicted many years ago, "The problem of the 20th century will be the problem of color." No one could have imagined how accurate those words would turn out to be. No problem facing us is more important than the problem of the Negro in American society. It is not only important in itself; it raises other questions that touch the meaning of our history and the society we have been raised in.

The relation of white and colored people is not only the most important national issue, it is a world issue. Scores of new nations have been born in the past twenty-five years, nations whose populations are almost entirely nonwhite. The communists, especially the Chinese, have drawn a picture of the future as a struggle between the white and colored races. They expect to lead the colored peoples in this struggle (though the Chinese show racial prejudices as strong as anyone's).

The United States, meanwhile, is working painfully toward a society in which people of all races, religions and nationalities can play an effective part. *We do not now have this kind of society.* To pretend we do only makes the problem worse. We do not know yet how we are going to achieve it. (Almost certainly no one solution is going to be enough). England, Brazil and other nations are working in their own ways toward the same goal. They have not achieved it either.

Yet the problems of race relations have never been closer to a solution than now. Every reader of this book is likely to have a part in that solution . . . or that failure.

1

THE STRUGGLE WITHIN

WHEN ERNEST GREEN and a few other Negro boys and girls were admitted to Central High School in Little Rock, Arkansas, white parents lined the streets and jeered at the Negro children. White students at first refused to go to class with them; then they taunted them or refused to speak to them. Armed National Guardsmen patrolled the high school corridors for many weeks before everyone settled down to work. That was in 1957.

A year later, Ernest Green was the first Negro ever to graduate from Central High. Fourteen of his white classmates wrote their goodbyes in his yearbook. "I have admired your courage this year," one wrote, "and I'm glad you made it through all right."

"I have enjoyed having home room with you this year. Your friendship has meant a lot to me."

"I really admire you, Ernest. I doubt if I could have

done half so well had the circumstances been reversed." [*]

Difficult decisions had to be made during those months. Ernest and his family had to decide whether to go on in the old, comfortable way, or to risk everything for the chance of a better future. The white students had to decide whether to accept their Negro classmates, or join the rest and snub them. Teachers had to decide between personal feelings and professional duty.

In Mississippi, a lady was told by her neighbors to fire the Negro couple who had worked in her home for thirty years. Civil rights workers had persuaded the couple to register as voters. The neighbors felt the Negroes ought to be taught a lesson: there was no place in this town for Negroes with "fancy notions" about voting.

But the lady who had been their employer for so long refused to fire them. Soon her neighbors stopped talking to her on the street. Her account at the store was closed. Finally she was no longer welcome at her church. When she was interviewed in her home, this southern lady said, "I honestly don't believe in equal rights for Negroes. But this couple has been loyal to me for thirty years and I feel like I ought to be loyal to them."

Again, there were hard decisions to make. The

---

[*] Ernest Green later attended Michigan State University, then went to New York City to help Negro boys prepare for jobs that had formerly been closed to them, as plumbers, carpenters and electricians.

woman and her neighbors had to decide which was more important, loyalty to friends or the ideas of white supremacy they had always accepted. The Negro couple had to decide whether voting was more important than risking their job and embarrassing their friend and employer.

New York City Negroes disagreed about how to make the public see their problem. One group wanted to picket the public schools and disrupt school board meetings in order to protest the fact that most Negro pupils in that northern city attend all-Negro schools. Another group was against this boycott; they preferred to work more quietly, in meetings with officials.

There were long discussions. Speakers for the first group said, "It is time we Negroes stopped worrying about what our white neighbors think. It is time we acted on our own!" The other group accused the leaders of the boycott of being more interested in headlines than they were in the schools.

The boycott took place, but not all Negro families supported it. Some white people were angered by it; others approved. Again, people had to think carefully about what was the most important to them. They made their decisions as parents, as friends, as citizens, not simply as Negroes or whites, northerners or southerners.

The race problem in our country is not an issue between good people and bad people. It is not an issue between North and South. It is not even an issue between Negroes and whites. These are too-easy explanations that make understanding more difficult. The real race problem is a struggle *within* white and Negro groups, *within* the South and North, *within* our political parties, churches, labor unions, clubs, fraternities and professional organizations. It goes on, in fact, within every person who thinks.

There are honest and dishonest people on both sides. There are segregationists in the North and integrationists in the South. There are still many white people at work in the civil rights movement. There are Negroes who favor separation of the races as much as any member of the Ku Klux Klan. And there are confused people on all sides.

Race discrimination never did start at the Mason-Dixon line. It is almost as strong in the North as in the South. Only the pattern is different.

In the South, until about 1965, segregation by race was enforced by local law and custom. Negroes were not permitted to use the same parks, restaurants, churches and other public places as whites. All bus and train stations had separate waiting rooms and rest rooms, marked "White" and "Colored." Negroes sat in the rear of buses and in special sections of movie theaters. They did not enter the front door of a white person's home (though inside they might prepare the food and take care of the children). There were separate schools and separate textbooks for black children; only the best Negro students got beyond the elementary grades.

If a Negro was willing to "keep his place," he might

live comfortably enough with his white neighbors. But no matter how well he might do, he was still called by his first name all his life (possibly with a courteous "Uncle" or "Doctor" attached).

Most of this had changed by 1970, but not all. School buildings are desegregated, but often classrooms are not. Restaurants are legally open to all, but bars may not be. Parks are no longer restricted to whites, but many public swimming pools are strangely shut down. Southern segregation is crumbling, but the remnants of it vary from place to place. In some cities there are black policemen. In one city it may be understood that they can arrest only Negroes; in another they can make arrests without regard to color. In one town motels may welcome Negro travelers; in another they may offer only insults.

In the North, segregation has never been supported by law, but it exists in fact and seems to be getting worse as Negro population grows. Most Negro families live in run-down "colored neighborhoods" called ghettos because they are unable to buy or rent in better parts of town. No law says they must live there, but no effort of theirs can get them out. This is called *de facto* segregation; it is more thorough in Chicago or Philadelphia than in southern cities like Charleston or New Orleans where white and Negro neighborhoods have been mixed for generations.

Since most northern Negroes live in the same neighborhoods, their children are likely to attend all-Negro schools. During the ten years after the Supreme Court declared segregation in public schools to be illegal, *de facto* segregation in northern city schools actually increased. According to a report made for the New York City Board of Education, 78 public schools that had formerly been mixed found in 1963 that over 90% of their pupils were Negro or Puerto Rican. This had not happened on purpose; while black and Puerto Rican population grew, white families were moving to the suburbs or sending their children to private schools.

There is more freedom for the Negro in the North, but few skilled jobs are open to him. Northern whites will call him Mister, but no matter how successful he becomes, a Negro will find it difficult to find a place for his family to live outside the ghetto.

To many Negroes, the southern way seems more comfortable and familiar. "At least we know where we stand," they say. But tens of thousands still move north and west, looking for new opportunities as Americans of all races have done. Before the Civil War, only about one Negro in ten lived in the North. Now the figure is more than one in three.*

The problem of race has become a national problem, not just a southern one. People in the North can no longer sit back and say, "Let them worry about it down there." People in the South can no longer say, "You stay out of our problem."

---

* The census of 1960 showed for the first time that a northern state—New York—has a larger number of Negroes than any other state. Of course many southern states still have a higher *percentage* of colored population.

Newspaper stories and television pictures of shootings and demonstrations make it seem as though there were a kind of war going on between the races. This is the easiest and most dangerous explanation of America's racial problem. Violence between the races makes big news but it is a very small part of the story. It is much less important than the struggle of white people and Negroes to *see* each other clearly.

For 300 years, the Negro has been slave and servant and the white man has been master. It is hard for either to see the other—or himself—in any other kind of relation. If, now and then, a white person meets a Negro lawyer, architect or teacher, he may find it hard to know how to act. A Louisiana politician complained about a television program produced in New York because it showed Negroes as cowboys. "Now everybody *knows* there was never such a thing as a colored cowboy!" he said. But there was and is such a thing. It just doesn't fit into the picture we carry in our heads.

For some people, the idea of a Negro voting or sitting down to dinner with white friends is just as unthinkable as a Negro roping steers.

This way of deciding about a whole group of people —according to our own ideas, instead of their worth—is called *prejudice*. No one is without some kind of prejudice. The word means to pre-judge; it is a short-cut way of dealing with people different from ourselves by fitting them into groups and treating them as though all the people in a group were just alike.

Prejudice can be aimed at any group we do not

know very well: people of other nationalities, other religions, other professions, even other parts of the country. (One of the things that complicates the race problem in America is northern prejudice toward southerners, and vice versa.)

Prejudiced notions about the Negro are too many to
count. "Negroes are lazy." "Negroes are devoted servants." "Negroes like living all in a heap." "Negroes are
wonderful musicians." Good or bad, these are all prejudiced opinions. And all are false.

The man who believes in the superiority of the white
race claims that his opinion is the result of a real fact:
that Negroes are *not*, on the average, the equal of
whites. Discrimination against the Negro is therefore
perfectly natural and absolutely necessary.

"Southerners are far less prejudiced than northerners," says Carleton Putnam in a booklet called *Race
and Reason*. If prejudice really does mean judging before getting the evidence, "the South has far more evidence, far more experience, concerning the Negro than
the North. And hence it is the North that is pre-judg-
ing when it tells the South what it ought to do about
the Negro problem."

But, it can be asked, how many people, even in the
South, really know the Negro? We only know the
Negro we have created—mostly hired men, elevator
operators and shoe-shine "boys." Even a colored minister, teacher or businessman is not likely to be invited
into a southern home, or otherwise treated as an equal;
can we say, then, that we really know him?

If prejudice against the Negro is "natural," if the

Negro is "obviously inferior," why don't we find the same prejudice everywhere? Why is it that in France, for example, Negroes are accepted without question and a Negro was for many years president of the French Senate?

The difference, segregationists say, is that in France —and in northern and western states—Negroes are a tiny minority, while in some parts of the South they outnumber the white population. A South Carolina senator explains, "Segregation exists in the South not merely because we prefer it, but because we *must* maintain it."

So it seems that segregation is not a natural reflex but a defense against a threat that is supposed to exist. The habit of segregation is rooted in a time when most American Negroes or their parents had recently come from a "primitive" life in Africa. Habit became law after the Civil War when southern whites were frightened by several million ex-slaves suddenly freed and given political rights.

Those times are far behind but the habits linger. For generations, white people kept them up because they made life comfortable and profitable. Negroes kept them up because it was easier and safer to do so. Now things are changing. Some white southerners accept these changes and even welcome them. Others resist at every step, but once the change is established they tend to accept it.

Every black person over 20 remembers the humiliation of being ordered to the back of a bus, or out of a restaurant. Negroes have been beaten and killed for stepping over the lines of segregation. Several thousand have been hanged or burned to death by lynch mobs for real or imagined crimes against white persons. Leaders of the civil rights movement have been shot by snipers, their homes and churches bombed. In May, 1971, a popular Drew, Mississippi, high school senior named Jo-Etha Collier was shot to death from a passing car. Her killers were "getting even" for a voter registration project that was going on in their town. Jo-Etha had just graduated that day from Drew High School, with honors.

Prejudice does not always take the shape of violence. In the traditional southern view, the Negro is ignorant, lazy and good-natured. He needs the white man's help. William Alexander Percy, in his novel *Lanterns on the Levee,* explains it this way:

> . . . the black man is our brother, a younger brother, not adult, not disciplined, but tragic, pitiable, and lovable; act as his brother and be patient.

This kind of prejudice can best be seen in a southern courtroom. A Negro who commits a minor offense, or a crime against another Negro, is let off easily. A judge may be heard to say, "Now Ben, you go home and see you don't do that again." As long as his offense is not against a white person, the southern Negro is treated like a naughty child. Petty theft, knife fights, drunkenness and desertion of wife and children are expected of Negroes. Southern whites shrug and say, "Well, that's the way they are, you know."

Many southerners are proud of their relations with the Negroes they know. "We give them clothing, take care of them when they're sick or in trouble. They're like part of the family," they tell visitors. One southern student defended segregation with perfect seriousness because "it gives us a chance to be kind to Negroes."

Negro leaders protest against this kind of prejudice, too. They see that it can be more damaging to their people than outright hatred, because it encourages them to be dependent and irresponsible.

Some friends of the Negro cause say that everyone should be "color-blind" in dealing with people. In other words, color should make no difference at all. A young Negro actress made this point in an interview with a newspaper reporter. "I have so often wanted to rush up to people and grab them by the shoulders and say, 'Look at *me*. Never mind my color. Please, just look at *me!*'" Many Negroes feel the same way. They want to forget their color, since it has always been used against them. Some of the movies starring Sidney Poitier, or the television series, "Julia," seem bent on proving that Negroes are just white folks with black skins.

This is a comfortable idea. To talk about racial or other groups as though they were all just alike, or should be, can be a kind of prejudice in disguise. Think about it: if you don't want to think of Negroes as "different," that means that you really want to think of them as white. Negro novelist John O. Killens is one of those who feel it important for Negroes to be different.

"White people still want their Negroes to have white insides under their black skins," he says, "but they won't find them any more. Negroes are recovering their racial identity, their pride in being black, and don't want to imitate the white man."

Still, many Negroes have come to share the prejudices of white people against them. All they know of themselves and their past is what white people have told them. "White is right. If you're black, keep back," the old saying goes. Light-skinned Negroes look down on those with darker skins. Negro mothers still discourage their children by telling them, "Niggers got no business going to college. That's a white man's world." When a Negro businessman took over a hamburger franchise in Cleveland, two black workers quit; they didn't want to work for a black boss.

Some young Negroes use prejudice as an excuse for doing nothing, for quitting school, for not caring. "Why should I bother?" they want to know. " 'Whitey' makes the rules and he isn't going to give me a chance."

Many other minority groups in America—racial, national or religious—have suffered from prejudice and discrimination: Jews, Quakers and Catholics, Poles, Irish, Mexicans, Chinese, Germans and others. Most of these have overcome their difficulties. The Negro still lags behind. "Doesn't this *prove* that the black race is inferior?" says the segregationist. Even people who sympathize with the Negroes have begun to ask, "Why all this fuss? Why should everything be made easier for *them?*"

Because, say leaders of the civil rights movement, no other minority has suffered 200 years of slavery. No other group has been set apart by law and identified as inferior. Except for the Chinese, the others have been able, because of their white skin, to slip into the stream of American life.

Prejudice against the Negro has been hardened into political and social institutions. It has been defended with scientific theories, historical legends and Biblical quotations. Until very recently, our history books said nothing about the part played by Negroes in the growth of America. Newspapers reported little about Negroes except crime stories and the doings of a few famous athletes and entertainers. In movies, Negroes were shown only as servants, criminals or comic characters.

For the first time, the American Negro is being looked at as a person—a black person. Only now is it being accepted that the ideals of American democracy apply to the Negro as well as to other men.

So the race problem is not just a matter of the way white people look at black people. It has to do with the way black people look at themselves, and at whites. It has to do with the way white Americans look at themselves and at the things they say they believe in.

At the first meeting of a class in black history, we discussed what we hoped to get from four months of studying the black experience in America. Black students naturally expressed the hope that the whole class would begin to appreciate the Negro past. A few added, "We don't know anything much about ourselves, except for slavery and Booker T. Washington."

A typical white response was, "I think we need to understand them better, what they want and so on." That was nice, of course, but it still reflected the idea that "we" white Americans have to understand "them," the nonwhite group outside. There was no hint at this first meeting that perhaps whites could learn about *themselves* in a black history course. No notion yet that it is not a problem of "us" understanding "them" but of an America which has always included both "us" and "them" and which would not be what it is without both. We came to this idea only after many weeks. (We will come back to it in Chapter 12.)

The race problem is a struggle to understand *what America and the Negro mean to each other*. This is what President Johnson—a southerner—was talking about when he spoke to the nation on March 15, 1965, during the "vote marches" in Selma, Alabama. The issue of equal rights for American Negroes, he said, touches "the secret heart of America itself."

> And should we defeat every enemy and should we double our wealth and conquer the stars, and still be unequal to this issue, then we will have failed as a people and as a nation . . .
>
> There is no Negro problem. There is no southern problem. There is no northern problem. There is only an American problem.

2

COLOR AND HISTORY—I

"This is a white man's country . . . The Negro
had nothing to do with the settling of America."
*Gov. Prentice Cooper
of Tennessee, 1940*

THE FIRST NEGROES arrived in the Virginia colonies in
1619—a year before the Pilgrims' landing at Plymouth.
Historians are very curious about these first Afro-A-
mericans and the attitude of the white settlers toward
them. Were these black men considered as slaves, or
merely as "servants" like so many whites who were
coming to the New World with only their labor to
offer? Were the restrictions on them different from
those placed on white servants? Did they finish their
term of service and become free, as many white servants did?

When did black servants come to be thought of as a separate class, to be enslaved for life? Why?

The answers to these questions are hard to find in the 16th century records. But they are important because they help to answer a basic question that is very much alive today: Is the racism of American society a permanent thing, or can it change with changing circumstances?

For a long time it was assumed that white colonists treated Africans as subhumans destined for slavery, from the very first. That seemed to mean that feelings of white superiority are so deep, so "natural" in Americans that they would probably never change.

But research is beginning to show that blacks were at first treated not much differently than other immigrant-servants of that time. Laws to segregate, control and finally enslave Negroes for life were not put into effect until about 80 years later, when economic circumstances seemed to demand it. We may never know much about the 20 or so Africans who were landed at Jamestown by a Dutch trader in 1619, but we do know that there were free, land-holding Negroes in Virginia as early as 1630.

This seems to say that "racism" changes with circumstances. If that is so, there is hope that it can be made to lose its force (if not disappear entirely) by changing the circumstances.

Unfortunately the *facts* of history are often less important than what people *think* has happened in the past. The Tennessee Governor who made the statement at the head of this chapter obviously believed that Negroes have always been slaves and that they did nothing on their own to help build the country. This is what he had been taught. So when a delegation of Negroes came to him in 1940 to ask that some of them be placed on local draft boards, the Governor refused. His decision, based on ignorance, helped to produce the bitterness and unrest that exploded later on.

It is more than curiosity that makes us examine the history of the black man in America. A better knowledge of the past helps us to make right decisions now and in the future.

Almost all American Negroes can look back to one or more ancestors who were slaves. Slavery is the most important fact in the history of the Negro in America. All of us, white and black, are still affected by the fact that for two centuries some Americans held other men as property.

Not all Negroes were slaves, however. Free Negroes came to America with the first explorers—with Columbus, Balboa and Cortez, with Ponce de Leon and De Soto. Negroes were among the first pioneers who settled in the Mississippi Valley. One, a French-speaking Negro named Joan Baptiste Pointe du Sable, came from Haiti through Louisiana and up the Mississippi River; the trading post he founded near Lake Michigan grew to be the city of Chicago.

Negroes set themselves up as farmers, carpenters, teamsters and blacksmiths in colonial America. They owned land and small businesses in the North and in Virginia, the Carolinas and Louisiana. Some even owned slaves.

As not all Negroes were slaves, not all whites were free. Thousands of poor immigrants from England, Ireland, Germany and elsewhere signed papers called *indentures* and came to America bound for a time (usually seven years) to serve a master without pay. Historians say that three out of five white persons arriving in the American colonies were bound to this kind of labor. Many were practically slaves, for they were kept in debt and had to renew their indentures again and again. Others bought their freedom or ran off to set up for themselves, and were lost in the mass of the white population.

There were early attempts to enslave the native Indians. But the natives sickened and died in captivity, or ran away to rejoin their people.

Throughout the seventeenth and eighteenth centuries, hundreds of thousands of Negroes were bought from Arab traders and tribal chiefs in West Africa and carried to America in the crowded holds of small wooden ships. A great many of them died during the terrible crossing. Those who survived were sold at auction. Their price depended on age and strength. Husbands, wives and childen might be bought separately and never see each other again. Tribal leaders were separated from their people.

And so the Negro's whole way of life was shattered: his family, his tribe, his religion. He became "a man without a past." He began to learn a new way of life, as the property of his white master.

Most slaves were brought to southern ports because the growing of rice, tobacco and cotton in that section required a great deal of hand labor. The northern states, busy with trade and industry, had less need of slave labor. But slavery was known in the North too, for a time; there were slaveholders among the early settlers of Pennsylvania, New York and New England.

Negroes brought from Africa could not return to their people, could not disappear in the white population. Having been completely cut off from their own culture and being so easy to identify, they were the easiest to subdue and exploit. Eventually a black skin became the mark of the slave. The words "Negro" and "slave" came to mean the same thing. When the American colonies declared their independence, there were half a million Negroes in the population of roughly four million; only one in twenty was a free man.

In 1776, Americans obviously did not consider Negroes as fellow-citizens of the new nation. Most of the founding fathers owned slaves, though some—like Washington and Jefferson—were very troubled by it. They felt deeply that men who were fighting for freedom had no right to oppress others. Jefferson included in his draft of the Declaration of Independence a long paragraph damning slavery and blaming the "execrable commerce" (unfairly) on England. This passage was stricken out at the insistence of southern delegates to the Continental Congress. The Declaration said that "all men are created equal" but few at that time thought the statement referred to black men as well as white.

General Washington at first refused to accept Negroes into the Continental army, but many of the state militia did accept them. After the British had had some success attracting slaves into their army with promises of freedom, Washington allowed Negroes to enlist. He encouraged slaveowners to free their slaves for the purpose of fighting for American independence. (Again, a change in circumstances made Americans behave differently.)

Most amazing of all, the great majority of Negro soldiers of the American Revolution fought in units made up mostly of white men. A Hessian officer fighting for the British observed that "no regiment is to be seen in which there are not Negroes in abundance: and among them are able-bodied, strong, and brave fellows." Apparently there was less segregation in the Continental army than there was in the American forces of 1917 and 1944!

After independence had been won, there was a strong movement to free former slaves. Most northern states ended slavery at this time. In 1787 the Congress prohibited slavery in the new territories north of the Ohio River.

But slave-holding was already deeply woven into the life of the new nation. Yankee shipowners continued to profit from the slave trade until the importation of Africans was made illegal in 1808—and even afterward.

New England textile-makers were eager to buy southern cotton at the lowest prices. So, while slavery as a legal institution continued only in the South, the North bears a share of the responsibility. The entire nation grew on the profits of slavery and the slave trade.

What was slavery like? Those who opposed it said it was thoroughly wicked and cruel, imposed by the whip and the pistol. Those who defended it said that it gave the primitive African his first taste of civilization, that it protected him, fed him and taught him religion. In either case, slavery meant that some men were the property of others.

There is no easy way to describe what the life of a slave was like. There were as many kinds of slavery as there were owners of slaves. A family might own only one or two slaves and these might be almost part of the family. The owner of a large plantation might have a hundred slaves or more, and he—or his hired overseer —might treat them with no more care than he gave his mules.

There was a great difference, too, between field slaves and household slaves. Field slaves were likely to live in crowded log shanties and be fed just enough corn meal and salt herring, peas and pickled pork to keep them working. Since the master had invested money to buy his slaves, he had some interest in their health; but slaves might be maimed or even killed for disobedience. When a field hand fell ill or was hurt, a doctor was rarely called since it was believed that "a nigger will get well anyway."

House servants were brought up with the family and lived in the "Big House." Every child of a slaveholding family had a Negro "Mammy" who was often closer to him than his own mother, and Negro playmates were his dearest friends. Elderly Negro servants were often called "Aunt" or "Uncle" and treated with great respect; it was they who ran the household, prepared meals, nursed the sick, scolded the other servants and even the white children when they were naughty.

House slaves might be taught to read and write (though this was against the law in some states). They might go with the master on his visits to town and learn something of business. They might be present when the mistress played on the piano or the master read aloud in the evening. They became much more cultivated and well-mannered than poorer whites. And of course they looked down on the field Negroes who lived in the shanties behind the Big House.

The difference between house servants and field hands had important effects. House servants often became devoted to their white owners and wanted to adopt their way of life. These were the "faithful old darkies" and the "good Negroes" that southerners like to remember. Their children and grandchildren had a better chance to get ahead. Most of the leaders of the Negro people came from this privileged group. The field slaves were ignorant and sometimes rebellious. In general, it is their descendants who have stayed on the land or filled the city slums.

House slave or field slave, the Negro knew he was

another man's property. He developed the habits of a slave: he became lazy, dependent, and clever at "getting around" the white man. He lied to his master, flattered him and agreed with him, just to stay out of trouble. To anything the white man might say, he replied, "Now ain't dat so?" He taught these habits to his children.

Family life was hardly known among slaves. It was important, of course, that slaves have children, for this added to the master's wealth. But slaves were not allowed to marry in the usual way; those that lived as husband and wife might be separated at any time if one of them was sold. Even the most treasured house servant knew that if times got bad and the family needed money, he might be sold away.

Some slaves were contented with their lot and even took pride in it. Jupiter Hammon, who was owned by a family on Long Island in New York, made a speech to the Negroes of that state urging them to hard work and patience. "For my own part," he said, "I do not wish to be free; for many of us who are grown up slaves, and have always had masters to take care of us, should hardly know how to take care of themselves."

Other slaves rebelled, burning plantations and killing their masters. Some killed themselves rather than live in slavery. Many more ran away—over 100,000 in the 50 years before the Civil War.

But most slaves expressed their feelings in other ways, especially in religious devotion and in music. Their joy expressed itself in the rhythms that we now call "jazz." Their sorrow and bitterness were in the songs that later became the "blues." "Nobody knows the trouble I seen," they sang, and "We'll soon be free, the Lord will call us home."

For a time, very early in the 1800's, it seemed as though slavery might come to an end by itself. There had always been southerners opposed to it. William Binford of Virginia set his slaves free in 1782 because he believed that "freedom is the natural right of all mankind." Men who worked for wages felt that the free labor of slaves was unfair competition. During debates in 1832, members of the Viriginia Assembly called slavery "runious" and a "withering curse." In those days there were more anti-slavery societies in the South than in the North.

It was "King Cotton" who persuaded the South that slavery had to stay. Cotton growing became more important than ever in the 1840's and 1850's. English mills were beginning to hum and English merchants bid the price of cotton higher each year. More cotton meant more slaves. Since Congress had put an end to the importation of slaves in 1808, they became still more valuable.

Maintaining the slave system was like holding a tiger by the tail: it was dangerous to hold on, dangerous to let go. Southerners decided to hold on. Opposition to slavery died out in the South. Slave-owners were more anxious than ever to prove that it was inferiority that made the black man a slave, not slavery that made him inferior. They used any argument that came to hand, arguments that are still used in defense of segregation. It did not matter that some of these arguments contradicted one another.

Negroes were described as naturally ignorant, unable to learn anything but the simplest tasks. Yet slavery was defended as the best way to teach the black man Christianity and good manners.

The Negro was said to be satisfied with slavery and devoted to his master. But at the same time people warned of the danger that he might rise up and destroy the whites.

Negroes were said to be an inferior species, but at the same time they were prized for their strength, agility and endurance.

In any case, said the southern plantation owner, the slave had a better life than the northern industrial worker of those days who worked from dawn to dark for a few dollars and had to take care of himself. To the southerner, the northern way of living was greedy and impersonal, while his own way was cultured and easygoing. Southerners saw their way of life as a new version of ancient Greek society: a small, educated upper class devoted to the arts, to graceful living and to government, while slaves and artisans did the hard work.

Plantation homes in the South were often built in classic Greek style. These relics of the old days can still be seen. Their white columns and broad porches are shaded by great trees. Their rooms are panelled and floored with rare woods, furnished with fine silks and

linens, with gleaming tableware and crystal. Great
balls and suppers took place in these homes. Young la-
dies learned French and embroidery and music. Young
gentlemen learned history and a little Latin, how to
ride and shoot, to give orders and keep accounts. The
Negroes made everything comfortable. It was a beautiful life and it grew to be a legend for all white southerners, rich or poor. (You may have seen the legend on
film, in "Gone With The Wind.")

Actually, only a few southerners lived this way.
There were plenty of ignorant slave-owners who barely
knew how to sign their names. Less than one out of
four southern families owned any slaves at all. Nearly
half of these owned five or less. Some had small farms
and rude houses and worked side by side with their
slaves and hired hands in the field. Others owned no
land at all, but farmed tiny plots for which they paid by
giving the owner part of what they grew. And of
course there were towns and cities where people lived
by trade or banking or small manufacturing.

It was the great plantations, though, that gave the
Old South its strength, its culture and its pride. And it
was the Negro slave who made it possible. Is it any
wonder that southerners convinced themselves that
slavery was natural and right?

One thing stood in the way of this belief: there were
thousands of American Negroes who were *not* slaves.
These free Negroes lived and worked and had property
and families much like other people, went to their own
churches, published newspapers and held public meet-

ings at which they complained of the injustices suffered by their people.

Some free Negroes had never been slaves. Others
had gotten their freedom one way or another. Often a
master would write in his will that his favorite slaves
were to be free on his or his wife's death. Sometimes a
slave was allowed to work for himself a bit—perhaps as
a shoemaker or trader—and he might save up enough
money to buy himself or a relative out of slavery. Others simply ran away, northward across the Ohio River.
So the community of free Negroes grew. By 1860 there
were nearly half a million, about half of these in the
South.

The existence of free Negroes was upsetting to slave-
holders. If Negroes were "slaves by nature," how could
so many live without any master? Besides, free Negroes were a bad influence on those who were still enslaved, giving them the idea that they too might be
free. Some free Negroes helped slaves to revolt. Others
helped to guide runaways to freedom in the North or
in Canada. With the help of white friends, they set up
a system of secret routes and stopping-places called the
"Underground Railway."

In the North, Negroes were looked upon as a curiosity during the early years of the Republic. But as more
escaped slaves settled in the North, feelings changed.
The ex-slaves were not so well-bred as the free men of
color who had settled earlier. And there were suddenly
so many of them.

So, beginning about 1840, states in the North and

the South passed laws that put limits on the free Negroes. They might not meet together or be on the
street after a certain hour. They were forbidden to en-
gage in some professions. Their right to vote was taken
away in Pennsylvania and Tennessee, Indiana and
Maryland. They could not serve on juries, or even appear in court as witnesses except in cases concerning
Negroes. Even in New York and New Jersey, Negro
children had to attend separate schools. In some states
there was no school that Negroes could attend.

In the South, any colored person who could not
show papers proving that he was free was liable to be
sold as a slave. Some states required Negroes to leave
the state as soon as they were freed.

Some people thought they had an answer to the
problem that would be good for the Negroes and for
the country. It was their idea to send all of the colored
population, slave and free, back to Africa, or to some-
place in Central America or the West Indies. The
American Colonization Society was established to re-
settle Negroes in Liberia, Africa. But there were many
problems. The expense was tremendous. Besides, Negroes who had been born in America had no desire to
"go back" to a continent they had never seen. And of
course there was great objection from plantation owners who had no wish to have their laborers taken away
from them. Though the colonization scheme was supported by Adams, Jefferson and even Lincoln, it never
got very far.

The American attitude toward the free Negro was

summed up in the case of Dred Scott, who went to
court to claim his freedom on the ground that his master had taken him to live in the free territory of Illinois.
In a famous decision given in 1857, the Supreme Court
ruled against Dred Scott. Chief Justice Roger Taney
wrote that Negroes had "no right which the white man
was bound to respect. . . ." That was the way most
people, North and South, felt about it. This was a
white man's country. White men had torn it from the
wilderness (and from the red man), and white men
would run it.

While opposition to slavery died out in the South, it
grew to giant proportions in the North. The movement
for the end, or *abolition,* of slavery became the most
powerful political force of the time.

The abolitionists turned a whole armory of argument
against slave-holding. First, they said, it was un-Chris-
tian. While some people used the Bible to prove that
slavery was part of God's plan, abolitionists wrote
books like *The Bible Against Slavery,* to prove that it
was contrary to Jesus' teaching of universal brotherhood. Second, they began to insist that the spirit of the
Declaration of Independence be taken literally: if *"all
men are created equal,"* this must mean black men as
well as white.

Abolitionists argued that slavery was uneconomical.
Since the labor of slaves was so cheap, plantation owners did not bother to adopt modern methods of farming. Besides, slaves would never work as hard as paid
laborers. Slavery was also becoming a danger to the

peace, for much of the South lived armed and in fear of Negro uprisings.

Worst of all, the abolitionists said, slavery made the white man and the Negro equally brutal. The master became cruel and arrogant and the slave became a liar and a coward. Each saw the other at his worst. Abraham Lincoln saw this and said, "As I would not be a slave, so I would not be a master."

Some abolitionists were red-hot extremists. Slavery was evil and their battle against it was like a religious crusade. The battle would not end, they swore, until slavery was destroyed—even if the Union of the states were destroyed with it. Slavery was just as emotional a subject then as segregation is now. The New York abolitionist William Lloyd Garrison wrote in his newspaper *The Liberator:*

> On this subject, I do not wish to think, to speak, or write, with moderation . . . I will not retreat a single inch—AND I WILL BE HEARD.

He was mobbed in Boston for his views.

The abolitionist John Brown looked like a bearded Biblical prophet. Some said he was mad. Convinced that the only way to end slavery was to strike it dead, he resolved to arm the slaves of Virginia. On a Sunday night in October 1859, he and about 50 followers—many of them Negroes—raided the federal arsenal at Harpers Ferry, Virginia. The attack failed and John Brown was hanged. But he had frightened the slaveholders and electrified the North.

From that moment, it seemed that the quarrel over slavery could only end in war. When Lincoln was elected President by the anti-slavery Republican Party in 1860, southerners were convinced they would have to fight for their way of life. That way of life could not exist without the Negro slave.

Even as the South withdrew from the United States and went to war, there were southerners like Bishop Elliott of Savannah who insisted that slavery was a blessing for Negro and white alike. "We are fighting," he said, "to protect and preserve a race who form a part of our household and stand with us next to our children."

3

COLOR AND HISTORY—II

SEPTEMBER, 1895: Atlanta, Georgia was bright with flags and sunshine for the Cotton States & International Exposition. Thirty years after the close of the Civil War, the "New South" was proudly displaying its growth to the rest of the fast-growing nation. There were prize animals, agricultural machinery, cotton textiles from the new factories. There was a special section devoted to the progress of the southern Negro.

A Negro was among the prominent men who had organized the exposition. He was Booker T. Washington, principal of a school at Tuskegee, Alabama which had been founded a few years earlier for the training of Negro teachers. Washington was invited to be one of the speakers on opening day.

It was a hot day. There was a three-hour parade and many speeches before the black man's turn came. He rose to cheers from the Negroes in the crowd and a scattering of applause from the whites. He was very nervous, for this speech was a hard-won privilege and he felt that if he was not careful it might be the last public speech by a Negro in Georgia for years to come.

By the time Booker Washington sat down, he had made himself the most influential person of his race, acknowledged by whites—and by many Negroes—as the leader of the Negro people. Like all great political orations, his speech said what people were ready to hear.

> The wisest among my race understand that the agitation of questions of social equality is the extremest folly and that progress in the enjoyment of all the privileges that will come to us must be the result of severe constant struggle rather than of artificial forcing.

He did point out that the South needed the Negroes, for they were one-third of the population there; if they were not able to help pull the South upward, their weight would certainly drag it down. But Negroes should recognize that their best friend was the southern white and that the "ignorant and inexperienced Negro must start at the bottom and improve himself with the white man's help."

Meanwhile it was too soon to talk of social equality. Holding up his hand before the audience, Washington said: "In all things that are purely social we can be as separate as the fingers, yet one as the hand in all things essential to mutual progress."

The speech caused a sensation in the audience.

Handkerchiefs and parasols were waved; canes were flourished. An ex-governor of Georgia shocked some people by rushing across the platform to shake the speaker's hand, and others then did the same.

Thousands of telegrams poured in, some offering large fees for speaking engagements. But Washington turned them down rather than leave his work at Tuskegee. President Cleveland wrote him a letter of congratulations, and newspapers praised his speech. The Atlanta *Constitution* called it "the most remarkable address delivered by a colored man in America." A Chicago paper said, "He has done more for the improvement of the Negro in the South than has been accomplished by all the political agitators. . . ."

Of course, Washington's words would win no applause from Negroes today. He set the pattern of race relations that lasted until recent years. Negroes would be content to live apart if they could have a small share in the nation's growth. This meant going back a step. For people could still remember the time—just after the Civil War—when Negroes had sat in the legislatures of southern states and helped to write the constitutions under which these states were re-admitted to the Union.

Now, a Negro leader was admitting that his people were not ready to take part in government. Negroes had taken the wrong turning of the road, he seemed to say. They must go back and follow the other road, behind the white man. Maybe then the white man would help them to catch up.

The story of the American Negro between the Civil War and Booker Washington's speech contains the beginnings of the modern problem of segregation. But it is hard to get a clear picture of those beginnings. The period, known as the Reconstruction, has caused more arguments among historians than any other part of the nation's past. The passions of the war lasted for many years, and the whole country was changing so fast during these years that people found it hard to understand what was happening.

The war itself was ennobled—as far as wars can be —by high ideals on both sides. Both fought to preserve what they believed to be the true spirit of the Constitution. Slavery was not the issue, but it symbolized the issue: whether the states had the right to regulate their way of life as they wished—and, if necessary, to withdraw from the union they had created. To the defenders of the Union, it was a Civil War. To the men of the Confederacy, it was a War Between the States.

Negroes fought on both sides. After great argument, Congress allowed colored regiments to be organized in the Union forces. More than 38,000 Negro soldiers gave their lives for the cause of the Union. All of them marched in separate units and were commanded by white officers.

The Confederacy feared to put weapons into the hands of Negroes. But hundreds of colored men went to the war as servants to their masters in uniform and some of them carried arms.

President Lincoln did not begin with the purpose of

ending slavery, but of preserving the Union at any
cost. In his inaugural speech he had said:

> I have no more purpose, directly or indirectly, to
> interfere with the institution of slavery in the
> States where it now exists. I believe I have no
> right to do so and I have no inclination to do so.

He was not sure of solid support for emancipation in
the North. He was anxious not to lose the four slave
states that remained in the Union (Delaware, Maryland, Kentucky and Missouri).

Finally, after nearly two years of terrible and indeci-
sive fighting, Lincoln made public a Proclamation of
Emancipation. Any slave-holder still in rebellion
against the United States on January 1, 1863, would
lose his human property. This was mainly a military
measure; it freed no slaves at the time. In areas under
U.S. control, slaves might remain in servitude. In areas
controlled by the Confederacy, the federal government
had no power to enforce the proclamation and many
slaves never heard about it.

Even so, the announcement had a tremendous effect.
In the North, Negroes stood silently on that first of
January to mark the end of centuries of bondage. In
the South, those slaves that heard the news reacted in
various ways. Some went on just as before. Some
walked away, fled to the Union lines, or just sat down
and "retired." A coachman in Richmond went straight
to his master's room, according to the local paper,
"dressed himself in his [master's] best clothes, put on

his best watch and chain, took his stick, and returning to the parlor where his master was, insolently informed him that he might for the future drive his own coach."

Southern historians say that if Lincoln had delayed much longer, the South itself might have had the credit for freeing the slaves. Confederate leaders desperately needed the support of European nations, especially England, which purchased so much southern cotton. They also knew that there was strong feeling against slavery there. Late in the war, President Jefferson Davis of the Confederate States sent an envoy to England and France to offer a plan: the South would free all its slaves in return for official recognition of the Confederacy. But the war ended before agreement was reached.

For southerners of both races, the years after the war were like a roller-coaster ride: up and down, sometimes exciting, sometimes frightening. Southern writers say that at the end of the war the friendship between the races was never stronger. Southerners were proud of the loyalty of many Negroes. "Many a master going off to the war entrusted his wife and children to the care of his servants with as much confidence as if they had been of his own blood," one of them wrote. They felt this was a tribute to the whites' natural command of the Negro, and proof that slavery had not been as frightful as abolitionists said it was.

Ignorant ex-slaves had an idea that emancipation would bring the easy life, "forty acres and a mule" and reunion with their families. "We thought we was going to get rich like the white folks," one of them recalled.

> We thought we was going to be richer than the white folks 'cause we was stronger and knowed how to work, and the whites didn't, and they didn't have us to work for them any more. But it didn't turn out that way. We soon found out that freedom could make folks proud, but it didn't make 'em rich.

Many Negroes drifted back to work for their old masters as hired hands or sharecroppers. Others went west.

Neither white nor Negro really knew how tremendous were the changes that had been set in motion.

The South was wrecked by the war. Lincoln had promised that the federal government would act toward the revolted states "with malice toward none, with charity for all." After Lincoln's death, President Andrew Johnson extended this generous policy; he made it clear that the rights of Negroes were far less important than rebuilding the South and renewing its ties with the rest of the nation. Former Confederate leaders were allowed to return to important positions. Southerners campaigned for office on their record as war heroes, and in the Louisiana legislature former Confederate officers wore their gray uniforms.

To these men, "Reconstruction" meant just what it said: the rebuilding of the South and its old way of life. Slavery was gone. But white supremacy, they felt, must remain. It was the only thing that might be salvaged from defeat. So they defended it with heart and soul— and later with pistol and firebrand.

By the end of 1865 most southern states and towns had enacted "Black Codes" that set close limits on the Negroes' new freedom. Any person not employed might be arrested and fined. If he could not pay the fine, he might be hired out to anyone who paid it for him. The hiring out of Negro convicts became a new kind of slavery. In Mississippi no Negro could own farm land. More towns adopted a curfew, requiring Negroes to be off the street by dark. The Ku Klux Klan and other organizations began terrorizing Negroes to keep them from using their newly won rights as citizens.

In the North, people said that the southerners were behaving as though they had won the recent war, not lost it. There were rumors that slavery might be re-established. Northern industrialists, with an eye on Negro labor, did not want to see this labor controlled again by southern planters. Republican politicians who hoped to win the new Negro vote saw their hopes fade as Negroes were frightened away from the polls.

There had always been important men in the North who said that President Johnson had been too easy on the South. Now their voices grew louder. "Plow the ground again and sow new seed the better!" they cried.

So the Republican-dominated Congress turned its back on the President and began a reconstruction of its own. Historians call this the "Radical Reconstruction." Southerners call it "Black Reconstruction."

The South was divided into military districts under

the command of Union generals. No state could be
readmitted to the Union until it annulled the Black
Codes and approved a constitution that agreed with
the new Reconstruction Acts. No state could be re-admitted until it had approved the 14th and 15th amendments to the U.S. Constitution (although most northern
states were arguing fiercely over them).°

Men who had fought for the Confederacy were not
allowed to vote or hold office until they applied for
pardon or took an oath of allegiance; but Negroes were
freely registered, under the protection of federal bayo-
nets. The Freedman's Bureau opened schools and distributed food, clothing and legal help to Negroes. The
Union League organized Negro voters for the Republican Party, using secret rituals and nighttime meetings
just as the Klans did.

Southern historians have claimed that the South was
"under Negro rule" during the years of Radical Reconstruction. "The Negro was invested with absolute
power," according to one writer. "What was the result?
Such a riot of folly and extravagance, such a travesty of
justice, such a mummery of government as was never
before witnessed. . . ." Another describes the Georgia
legislature of the time as "a cross between a gambling
den and a colored camp meeting." Figures are pro-

° The 14th amendment extended to the freedmen the rights of
U.S. citizens. (See p. 82). The 15th amendment said that the
right to vote "shall not be denied or abridged by the United
States or by any state on account of race, color or previous con-
dition of servitude."

duced to prove the corruption and foolishness of these part-Negro legislatures.

Other historians disagree. Going back over the records, they find that there were no Negro governors and that Negroes never made up a majority of any legislature or convention. For a time there were more Negro voters than whites in the states of the old Confederacy, but white registration grew steadily as pardons were granted. The Reconstruction legislatures wrote many progressive laws which have remained in force ever since, including the establishment of a system of public schools.

The new Negro leaders came almost entirely from among the free colored population. Hiram Revels, who took the U.S. Senate seat formerly held by Jefferson Davis, was a minister educated in the North. Jonathan Gibbs, Florida's Negro secretary of state, was a graduate of Dartmouth College. John Roy Lynch had "stolen" an education by following the work of a white class that met just across the alley from his photography studio; he became speaker of the Mississippi House of Representatives and later a member of Congress. Robert Smalls, a Negro Congressman from South Carolina, was a war hero who had seized the Confederate ship "Planter" and delivered it to Union authorities. Francis L. Cardozo, South Carolina's state treasurer, had been educated in England and been a minister in Connecticut. These were outstanding men in a time when education was not so widespread as it is today. (President Andrew Johnson himself did not learn to write until late in life.)

In general, Negro leaders in the postwar South accepted the separation of the races. They were moderate in their demands and they petitioned Congress many times to permit former Confederates to re-enter politics. Many who were ignorant were anxious to learn. Beverly Nash, a former slave who sat in the South Carolina convention, said:

> I believe, my friends and fellow-citizens, we are not prepared for this suffrage. But we can learn. Give a man tools and let him commence to use them, and in time he will learn a trade. So it is with voting. We may not understand it at the start, but in time we shall learn to do our duty.

Dishonesty and misgovernment were no worse during the Radical Reconstruction than they were in northern states at the same period. All over the country, business was growing at a mad pace. The infamous Tweed Ring ruled New York City and scandals were making headlines everywhere, including the nation's capital.

Most southerners, however, felt that Reconstruction was more devastating than the war itself. They were resolved to stop it.

One by one, as southern states were re-admitted to the Union, ex-Confederate leaders set about to recapture the state governments. Pistols became a regular part of a gentleman's dress. The Ku Klux Klans grew to be the most powerful force in the South, so powerful that President Grant tried to outlaw them. But it was no use. More organizations sprang up: the Knights of the White Camellia in Louisiana, the White Line in Mississippi, the Knights of the Rising Sun in Texas, Pale Faces, White Leagues and '76 Associations.

Republicans, white and Negro, were whipped and warned to get out of the state or stay away from the polls. Members of the Union League and of the state militias were ambushed and shot. A habit of lawlessness began to take hold in the South. Soon it was impossible to keep enough soldiers and federal officials on hand to stop it.

Years later, on the floor of the U.S. Senate, "Pitchfork Ben" Tillman of South Carolina looked back on this desperate time and said openly, "We have scratched our heads to find out how we could eliminate the last one of them. We stuffed ballot boxes. We shot them. We are not ashamed of it."

While this was happening, the North was turning its attention to other things. Railroads were being built across the continent; oil was discovered in Pennsylvania and iron in Minnesota and Alabama. The country was pushing west again, as the Indians gave way. Silver and copper mining was begun. Businessmen were anxious to see relations with the South get back to normal, so trade and investment could go forward. Northern politicians needed southern support for problems that seemed more important than civil rights: the opening of the West, free coinage of silver, immigration from Europe, the Cuban revolt against Spain.

Most of the old abolitionists had died. People were getting tired of the "Negro problem." There was a feeling that southerners ought to be left to handle it in their own way. It was "their problem" after all; as late as 1900 only 10% of the country's Negroes lived in the North.

So the roller-coaster started down again for the Negro, faster than ever. Reconstruction ended formally in 1877 when President Hayes withdrew the last few troops from the South. Conservative Democrats were already in power in every state.

The hurried gains that the Negro had made were undone. State constitutions were rewritten again, this time with provisions that barred Negroes from public life. "Jim Crow" laws separated the races in every public place: there were separate sections in streetcars, trains and courtrooms, separate schools, parks and public toilets, even separate hospitals and cemeteries. The new legislatures spent as little as possible on Negro facilities. The Negro, being poor, paid little tax; so no one saw any reason to spend much state money on him.

This was the situation when Booker Washington spoke in Atlanta in 1895. The postwar experiment in Negro equality had been a failure. Whites in the North had pushed him forward faster than he could go. Whites in the South had held him back. Neither was very much concerned with the Negro as a person, but only with what could be gained by controlling him.

Because of so many mistakes, the races now grew further apart than ever.

In the North and the South, whites found it easy to convince themselves that the Negro was not really worth worrying about. Once again he was pictured as hopelessly inferior. This picture took many forms: "scientific" racial theories, sentimental memories of old plantation days, crude jokes, and caricatures of watermelon-eating darkies. Newspapers, books and all the best magazines showed the Negro as either a brute or a fool.

The kindest writer of the period was Joel Chandler Harris, who created the popular "Uncle Remus" stories. Uncle Remus was an old-time Negro with a picturesque way of talking. Here is what he had to say about education for Negroes:

> Hit's the ruinashun er dis country . . . Put a spellin'-book in a nigger's han's, en right den en dar you loozes a plowhand . . . What's a nigger gwineter l'arn outen books? I kin take a bar'l stave an' fling mo' sense inter a nigger in one minnit dan all de schoolhouses betwixt dis en de State er Midgigin.

All the while, some Negroes *were* getting an education. With help from the Society of Friends, the American Missionary Association and several northern foundations, many vocational schools and teachers' colleges were established. Some northern universities were admitting Negroes. A new generation of Negro leaders was being trained, men and women who would one day lead a new move toward freedom. (See Chapter 8.)

Negroes fought alongside Teddy Roosevelt's "Rough Riders" in the Spanish-American War of 1898. But that war brought several million more colored people under U.S. control—in Cuba, the Philippines, and elsewhere —and added to the white American's feeling of racial superiority.

In 1909, President Taft told Negro students at a North Carolina agricultural college, "Your race is adapted to be a race of farmers, first, last and for all time." In 1915, the year that Booker T. Washington died, 69 Negroes were killed by lynch mobs. Progress had been very slow along the road he had pointed out to the Negro in Atlanta 20 years before.

4

COLOR AND THE SCIENTISTS

I'm blue, black and evil, and I didn't make my-
self.

East Texas blues song

You could ship-wreck 10,000 illiterate white
Americans on a desert island, and in three weeks
they would have a fairly good government, con-
ceived and administered upon fairly democratic
lines. You could ship-wreck 10,000 negroes, every
one of whom was a graduate of Harvard University, and in less than three years . . . half of the
men would have been killed, and the other half
would have two wives apiece.

John Sharp Williams of Mississippi
in Congress, Dec. 10, 1898

It is easy for these gentlemen to taunt us with
our inferiority, at the same time not mentioning
the cause of this inferiority. It is rather hard to be
accused of shiftlessness and idleness when the ac-

cuser closes the avenue of labor and industrial pursuits to us. It is hardly fair to accuse us of ignorance when it was made a crime under the former order of things to learn enough about letters to even read the Word of God.

George H. White of N. Carolina
in Congress, Feb. 23, 1900

NEITHER OF THESE is a scientific statement. But both reflect a scientific controversy that lies behind many arguments on human rights. The first assumes that a person's behavior is ruled by the traits with which he is born, or his *heredity*. The other suggests that inborn traits are less important than the *environment* in which they grow.

This tug-of-war between heredity and environment runs through all of the following questions that scientists study: In what ways do races differ? Is one race "better" than another? Are the important differences built-in at birth, or built up as a child grows into an adult? Does the mixing of races produce stronger or weaker individuals? The answers are not always clear to scientists. But that does not stop other people from rushing to conclusions.

The idea of race itself is an example. In all the English language there is no other word more loosely defined and more freely used. Some scientists have divided mankind into two races, others into four, or 18, or 200, based not only on color but shape of head, or language group, hair form, stature or facial characteristics. However they do it, there is a fuzzy edge to the definition, "typical" characteristics that are missing in some individuals, or show up in some persons of another race.

The most obvious differences—like color—may be only a tiny fraction of the biological "recipe" for human beings. According to one study, more than 95% of the biological equipment of any human being is identical with all other human beings. How much difference the other 5% makes is an unanswered question.

It is generally agreed that pure races do not exist. Man has been wandering over the earth for too many generations to have kept his racial lines distinct. Almost 80% of American Negroes are of mixed Indian or white ancestry, according to anthropologist Melville Herskovits.

Many scientists call the whole idea of race a "myth," an unscientific idea. The "typical Negro," like the "typical American," is simply the imaginary sum of all the characteristics that we think of when we say "Negro" or "American." If this is true, statements about persons based on their race or nationality have a very limited meaning.

Such scientific opinions are fairly new. Most of the men who are today considered experts in the matter of race are working in fields that were unknown at the beginning of this century. The scientific arguments over "racial equality" are largely a dispute between older sciences, like biology and genetics, and the newer "social" sciences, especially anthropology, and social psychology. The former deal mostly with questions of heredity, the latter with environment.

It is the new anthropology that is most sharply criticized by segregationists. Anthropology (from the Greek *anthropos,* meaning man) is the study of the origins of men, and of their relation to the places where they live, and to one another. Anthropologists live among different peoples all over the world, learning their languages and customs, their ambitions and beliefs. In general, they have come to the conclusion that what look like inborn differences may actually result from the fact that each society has different ideas of what is important and proper, and teaches these ideas to its children. A Negro and a poor white brought up in the same neighborhood will be more alike than a Negro from Alabama and a Negro from Zambia.

More than any other man, Franz Boas was responsible for the growth of the new science. This German-American scholar taught at Columbia University for 40 years; his students have written most of the textbooks college students now use: Ruth Benedict, Otto Klineberg, Clyde Kluckhohn, Ralph Linton, Margaret Mead and others. Their work has convinced them that, in Boas' words, "Behavior is much more strongly influenced by outer conditions than bodily build." Not race, but culture shapes the personality.

This is a frankly equalitarian view. It is attacked as "wishful thinking" by those who hold to the strictly biological view that the most important traits of behavior are inherited.

Americans found it easy to accept new ideas about race during World War II. For we faced an enemy who made the "sacredness of pure race" a weapon of war and who killed whole populations of "inferior" people. People who remember Nazi racism still have a feeling of disgust for arguments of racial superiority. So—just as with abolitionism a century ago—emotion adds its weight to argument.

The battle between the old sciences and the new runs through all the arguments about racial equality. It will be enough to look at three of these arguments: 1) The Negro race is at an "earlier stage of evolution" than other races. 2) The Negro is "less intelligent" and "more prone to crime and immorality." 3) Race mixing "threatens the future of the nation." Do not be surprised if some of the evidence is contradictory—or if the same evidence is used to support opposite conclusions.

The origins of man and ancient civilizations: When a die-hard segregationist is asked how long he thinks it will take for the Negro to reach a level where integration might be acceptable, he will probably reply, "Never!" Then he may hazard a guess at "about 200,-000 years." He is not making a joke. He believes his guess to be scientific.

The earliest remains of *Homo sapiens,* or Man-as-we-know-him, are thought to be about 250,000 years old. These bits of jaw and skull were found in England and in Germany. Skulls of a more primitive ancestor known as *Homo erectus* have also been found. All the

remains of *erectus* found in Europe are older than
250,000 years. But in Africa some *erectus* bones have
been found from as recently as 30,000 years ago.

This has given rise to a theory that while *Homo sapiens* was developing in Europe and Asia, the more
primitive *Homo erectus* took refuge in Central and
South Africa and lived there without any further development until a much later time. In other words, Man-
as-we-know-him *may* have developed almost 200,000
years later in Africa than in other parts of the world.

To racists, this means that the white man has a
"lead" of 200,000 years over the Negro. This is only a
theory, of course, and most scientists agree that it is
based on too little evidence. Newer discoveries in East
Africa suggest that human development has gone on
there at least as long as anywhere else. It has also been
pointed out that the Negro is *less* primitive in some
physical characteristics than the white: the body-hair,
thin lips and straight hair of the white are more "ape-
like" than the hairless bodies, thick lips and hair form
typical of the Negro!

The lack of great African civilizations is used as
proof that the Negro race is less capable. It has always
been claimed that no Negro empire ever existed in Africa that could rival the ancient civilizations of the
Mediterranean world, or of China, Mexico or Peru.
The Negro, it was said, has no past.

Social scientists have begun to challenge these arguments, too. A civilization cannot be judged in compari-
son with other civilizations, they say, but only by its

own usefulness. If the African Negro (like the Inca of Peru) did not develop writing, it may not be because he was incapable of it but because he had no need for it. Africans became accomplished at other kinds of expression instead: singing, dancing and story-telling. There is evidence that iron-working was discovered in black Africa, and as scholars begin to take an interest in African history, we are hearing more about the powerful and well-organized kingdoms of the Zulus, of Ghana, Mellestine and Songhay that existed centuries ago.

In any case, the American Negro is not an African, but an American. If he visits Africa, he feels just as strange as any other American going there for the first time. The southern writer James McBride Dabbs reminds us that the culture of the American Negro *is* an American culture, "for we are the only people from whom the Negroes could have got it."

Brain size and intelligence: The question "Are Negroes as intelligent as whites?" has no meaning unless we know *which* Negroes and which whites, under what conditions, and what we mean by intelligence. The research done on this subject is confusing because these questions are not often answered.

A fairly clear problem, like the relative size of the brain of Negroes and whites, leads to results that seem to contradict one another, results that are then seized on to "prove" that colored children should (or should not) attend schools with whites. On one side, scientists have found that "the frontal lobes of the typical Negro are smaller and the cerebral cortex less wrinkled [that is, showing fewer patterns of use] than the typical white's." Other scientists have found "no significant racial differences between blacks and whites in the size or weight of the brain."

We may wonder how such disagreement on facts can exist among men whose business is the study of facts. Is somebody being dishonest? Probably not. On looking closer, it usually appears that the facts being studied by one scientist are not exactly the same facts the others are studying. Some experiments have dealt with African Negroes, some with American; some used brains of criminals (always more easily available for research); some studied one part of the brain, some another; some drew their conclusions from the averages, some from the extremes. It takes scientific training to see exactly what has been proved.

One group of scientists is not so sure the overall size of the brain is important. They point out that it is not size but efficiency that matters. And in both races, the frontal lobe (regarded as the seat of intelligence) occupies about 44% of the total weight of the brain. One conscientious scientist, often cited in racist literature, did find certain differences in the patterns of frontal lobes in whites and Negroes. But he was careful to add, "The significance of these differences will be better appreciated when more is known of the functions of the various parts of the brain." In other words, we do not yet know enough to judge the value of what we *do* know in this field.

If we are on such shaky ground in dealing with a clear-cut problem like the measurement of the brain, much more confusion is possible in discussing the relative "intelligence" of races. During the first World War, a series of tests was given to white and Negro draftees. Ever since then, segregationists and their opponents have both insisted that the results "prove" what they believe to be true.

There is no question that Negroes, on the average, did less well on those tests than whites; they have continued to do less well on similar tests. This shows, segregationists say, that Negroes are less intelligent.

But Negroes from certain northern states did far better than whites from certain southern states. Both Negroes *and* whites from the North did better than Negroes and whites from the South. This shows, say integrationists, that discrimination and poor education produce poor minds, regardless of race.

The figures on Negro crime and poverty, on drug addiction, school dropouts, illegitimate births, and so on, produce the same disagreement. Segregationists say they prove that the Negro has a "natural tendency to crime and immorality." Others say that slavery, segregation, and poverty are to blame. No one is more worried about these figures than Negro preachers and writers—and Negro parents who worry about their children.

Race mixing and intermarriage: "Every time a great civilization has lost the purity of its white blood," segregationists say, "it has gone down to destruction. It

happened with the Greeks, with the Egyptians, with
the Roman Empire." This argument has filtered down
from the writings of Count Gobineau, a Frenchman
who, in the middle of the last century, published an
Essay on the Inequality of Human Races. He con-
cluded that "all civilizations derive from the white
race, that none can exist without its help, and that a
society is great and brilliant only so far as it preserves
the blood of the noble group that created it. . . ." The
terrible threat in social equality for the Negro, as racists see it, is the "mongrelization of the white race."

On the other hand, historians tell us that the Egyptians, the Greeks and the Romans were themselves
"mongrel" peoples, the result of cross-currents of mi-
gration, trade and warfare that were sweeping the
world. Their periods of greatest advance came at the
very times when they were in closest contact with
alien peoples.

The British, or "Anglo-Saxons," are often held up as
the example of a pure and vigorous group. But Karl
Pearson, a British scientist, found traces of nearly
every race that had wandered across Europe: Irish,
Norman, Italian, Hun, Scandinavian, Frankish and
Russian.

Even the principles of livestock breeding are used in
arguments about human races. Segregationists point
out that "improvement of type comes only through the
careful selection of breeding stock, and the rigid separation of animals of dissimilar or undesirable characteristics . . . impressive evidence that segregation pro-

motes development and progress." Their opponents answer that the best breeds were originally produced by crossing various strains with desirable characteristics. In both plants and animals, the resulting hybrids are often the strongest and most useful breeds.

The real problem of race mixing for the southern white is not one of biology or of race pride. The real problem is emotional. It touches the most secret fears that men can have. Certain things are known, but not spoken of, by all southerners, black and white. It is known that white slave-holders often fathered children by Negro women. The relationship did not stop with the end of slavery. The *mulatto*, the "strange fruit" of this union, can be seen everywhere: light-skinned Negroes whose fathers or grandfathers were white.

Negro men have always known of this relationship. White women knew, too. The white man, fearing the revenge of the Negro, terrorized him to keep him from it. Feeling guilty toward the white woman, he put her on a pedestal and called her the "spotless flower of white womanhood."

Out of this dark brew of fear, guilt and hate a hideous specter arose: the specter of rape. Since shortly after the Civil War, accusations of rape against Negro men have been a spur to race hatred. True or false, the accusations have often resulted in a crime just as brutal, the lynching of supects by hanging, shooting or burning.

Psychologists see a similarity between this and the famous witch trials of colonial New England. Like all "witches" of Massachusetts, the "brute Negro" of Mississippi is chosen to be the symbol of what is most feared within ourselves. By killing him, we kill our own dark guilt. And if the witch is not wicked enough, or the Negro not sensual enough, we surround him with legends to make him more so. The witch, it was said, could fly through the air in a twinkling. The Negro, many whites believe, has sexual powers far beyond other men. We now know that one notion is as false as the other.

Still, it is a constant theme of racist literature. "The Negro, in so far as sex is concerned, is not immoral, he is simply nonmoral," says one pamphlet. "He merely follows his natural instincts." Thomas Nelson Page, the southern novelist, insisted that "the Negro does not generally believe in the virtue of women. It is beyond his experience." Negroes find a bitter irony in these remarks. They remember that for 250 years Negroes were forbidden to marry lawfully while they were encouraged to produce children as though they were livestock.

In the North, interracial marriage is a step that is full of difficulties. In the South, the subject is surrounded with taboos that make it almost unspeakable. At the bottom of every segregationist argument is the fear of intermarriage, of "race mixing" and "mongrelization." Putting white and Negro children together in classrooms is thought to be the first step in that direction. The fact that intermarriage is rare in the North, where it is not prohibited, does not seem to lessen this fear.

On one hand segregationists claim, "The Negro does not really want to mix with the white; he is happy with things as they are." Segregation is said to be one of nature's laws: bluebirds, after all, do not mate with mocking-birds, nor blackbirds with jays. On the other hand, every interracial marriage is heavily publicized by the southern press as proof of the terrible dangers of desegregation.

Fear has no logic. Science is built on logic. So, when science is dragged feet first into the race problem, it generally takes a terrible beating and the result is more confusion than before. The facts of race difference are only part of the problem in any case. The next three chapters examine how people *use* race for business or political gain, and how our laws and our churches reflect what people *think* and *feel* about race.

5

COLOR, MONEY AND POLITICS

> Them white folks are always telling me, "Isn't it
> wonderful the progress that's been made amongst
> your people. Look at Dr. Bunche!" *
> All I say is, "Look at me."
>
> Simple (*Langston Hughes*)

THE RACE PROBLEM in the United States grew up with
the country. It did not come late, as in England, where
large numbers of West Indian Negroes have only recently entered the country. It has not always remained
the same, as in South Africa or Rhodesia, where a
handful of white settlers have always controlled a large
majority of native Negroes. Instead, the relations of
whites and Negroes changed as the country changed.
Discrimination against the Negro minority has become
tightly woven into our economic and political life.

---

* Dr. Ralph Bunche, a Negro, Under Secretary General of the
United Nations, for Special Political Affairs, died in 1971.

Not everyone who profits from discrimination is white; not all who suffer from it are black. The same person may profit from it in some ways and suffer from it in other ways, often without knowing how this happens. If a "profit-and-loss" statement of discrimination were drawn up, it would be very complicated.

Of course segregation was begun by white men who believed it would protect and benefit them. "If you want to rise, keep the nigger down" is the way some people put it. This meant segregating him not only in schools, churches, neighborhoods and the rest, but holding him back from higher education, from ownership of property, from skilled jobs and from political power.

There were a few protesting voices in the early years of "Jim Crow" legislation, at the end of the nineteenth century. Thomas Jones, a governor of Georgia, saw a danger in depriving the colored people of the opportunity to get ahead. "If we do not lift them, they will drag us down," he said. Booker T. Washington put it another way: "You can't hold a man in a ditch," he said, "without staying down there with him."

In general white people have been willing to pay whatever it cost to keep the Negro down. Some of the costs were easy to see: millions of dollars spent for separate schools, separate waiting rooms in bus stations, separate parks, restrooms, elevators and even public drinking fountains. These were the first to go.

A less obvious cost of the Negro's inferior position is that of welfare services provided by government: unemployment insurance, aid to abandoned families and so on. A large share of these services goes to Negroes. Segregationists say this proves that Negroes are not responsible citizens, that they are a burden to the South and to the nation. Negroes answer, "If we are a burden, it is because you make us one. Negro citizens with jobs and businesses would pay more taxes and would not need so much help."

According to the U.S. Census, the average Negro in the United States earns about half as much as the average white. Men are twice as likely to have no job at all. Negro families are more likely to live in homes that are crumbling and rat-infested.

Many Negro mothers must work, taking care of white families while their own children "run loose." A Negro child is twice as likely to drop out of school, only half as likely to graduate from high school. It is hard for him to see why he should keep on, when most good jobs will be closed to him anyway. It is hard for him to feel like a responsible citizen when he is shut off from so much. "I got no country. I got no flag," said one 16-year-old boy in San Francisco when he was interviewed on television.

It does not matter whose fault this is. The results are costly to the whole country. That is why the government has declared a "war on poverty" and why this program is so important to both Negroes and whites.

There are other results of race discrimination that are still harder to see. These have a powerful effect on American politics and on the economy of our country.

After the post-Civil War years, southern states began to make it very difficult for Negroes to vote. A poll tax had to be paid. Complicated rules were set up for registration. As recently as 1956, Mississippi passed a law requiring voters to give a written explanation of any section of the long state constitution chosen by the registrar. It was left up to the registrar to decide if the explanation was a good one. As a result, about half the state's Negro voters were dropped from the lists. In many counties throughout the South, Negroes who try to register are kept standing in line for days, or disqualified because they have not dotted their i's or crossed their t's.

Fraud and threats are used, too. It is not many years ago that Mississippi Senator Theodore Bilbo said publicly, "The best way to deal with the nigger is to visit him the night before the polls open." Negroes who do register to vote may find themselves fired from their jobs or run out of town.

All this looks good to whites who fear "black domination." But men who study southern politics point to a curious result of the effort to keep the Negro "out of politics": the votes of white people lose their importance too.

Voters in the North and West talk about national and world issues. They have a chance to vote for men who have ideas on these issues. But in the South, election campaigns have usually been a contest to see which candidate is loudest in support of white supremacy. Out of 14 candidates for governor of Alabama in

1958, not one dared to suggest that the rights of Alabama Negroes should be discussed. Any who may have
wanted to, did not dare to say so.

The race issue in the South has nearly destroyed the
two-party system on which American politics is based.
Until very recently, there was only one political party
of any importance in the South: the Democrats. The
Republican Party was hated because its leaders had
imposed the stern Reconstruction policies after the
Civil War. So it became a "dummy" party that existed
only in name. Southerners generally accepted this as
part of the cost of white supremacy. But sometimes
there was a complaint, like this editorial that appeared
in the Columbia (S.C.) *Record* in 1948:

> All white persons in South Carolina are not of
> one mind on the great national issues. But by
> making the Democratic party of South Carolina
> the white party, South Carolinians have smoth-
> ered these differences and disfranchised for every
> practical purpose everybody who didn't go along
> with the national Democratic party.

Even within the Democratic party, southerners have
been kept from taking part in important issues because
they were tied to the issue of race. In 1948, several
southern states walked out of the Democratic convention and ran their own man for President on a "States'
Rights" ticket.* In this way, they deprived voters in

---

* The States' Rights candidate, Sen. Strom Thurmond, joined
the Republicans in 1964, because the Republican candidate opposed civil rights legislation.

those states of the chance to cast a ballot for one of the two major candidates; the name of President Harry S. Truman did not appear on the ballot because he was "too liberal" on the race issue. President Johnson got the same treatment in 1964.

Since there are so few real issues, many southern whites do not bother to vote at all. This pleases some politicians, for it leaves more political power to them. These men, usually representing the most extreme point of view on race, are elected year after year, not only to local offices but also to the Congress. There they rise automatically, because of their long service, to control of important committees. And so it often happens that laws of great importance to the country are blocked by men who are elected by a tiny proportion of the voters in their district, men who have no interest in national and international issues.

In this way, most white southerners lose their share in the political life of the nation, while a few take far more than their share. Comforted by the feeling that they are running things and "keeping the Negro in his place," southerners do not notice that their own political power has been whittled away. All this happens because of the Negro; he, without voting at all, is the most important political figure in the South.

Now, Negroes have begun to exercise their own political power. In spite of the obstacles, they are registering in greater numbers than at any time since Reconstruction. A Voter Education Project, aided by several national organizations, is helping them. Student

workers help to fill out the complicated forms and prepare for the reading tests and other requirements. Between 1960 and 1968 nearly two million Negro voters
were added to the lists in southern states. The Voting
Rights Act of 1965 make it much more difficult to deprive anyone of his vote because of race. Negroes cast
more than one-fifth of the southern vote in the 1968
elections and the number is growing.

As the Negro vote grows in the South, white candidates are toning down their racial arguments. Large
cities like Atlanta and New Orleans have begun to approach complete desegregation, in part because of
black votes. The new strength of the Republican Party
in the South is partly a reaction to the growth of the
Negro vote.

In 1970, almost the only major candidate to make an
outright racist appeal was a Republican running for
the governorship of South Carolina. He was defeated
by John West, who promised a "color-blind administration." A new crop of progressive governors took office
that year in Georgia, Virginia, Florida and Arkansas.
Black votes helped to elect them.

Equally important is the rapid rise in the number of
Negroes elected to public office. In the entire country
in 1967 there were only 475 elected black officials; in
April of 1970 there were four times as many. The number is still very small (less than 1% of all elected officials) but it includes county clerks and sheriffs, over 20
mayors from Michigan to Mississippi, New Jersey and
California, a dozen Congressmen and the first black

Senator since Reconstruction, Edward Brooke of Massachusetts.

Ironically, a good deal of this black political power comes from the very racial discrimination that keeps Negroes bunched together in black communities. Chicago's west side and the ghetto neighborhoods of Cleveland, Newark and Los Angeles have black voting majorities greater then Fayette, Mississippi or Greene County, Alabama. Segregation encourages black political power, and as voter registration grows many more communities are going to have black officials. The population of the South is still 20% black; Negroes are a majority in 101 southern counties. Yet in early 1971 they controlled only four of these counties and held 40 of the 1805 seats in southern legislatures.

Most Negroes who hold elective jobs are not just representatives of the black community, however. Men like Senator Brooke, Mayor Carl Stokes of Cleveland, or Georgia legislator Julian Bond attract white voters too. Their jobs require them to be spokesmen for the entire community, not for the Negro alone. Through them we are learning something about the possibilities of sharing power.

Progress has been far slower in the matter of jobs and income. This is a more complicated problem. There is no one place to take hold of it and shake it, as the political situation was shaken by pressing for voter registration.

Between the Civil War and the first World War, the

United States changed rapidly from a farming nation to an industrial nation. Most of the change took place in the North. Factories and railroads made new jobs. In the growing cities, new ideas circulated more rapidly than in farm areas, through books, newspapers and public meetings.

Change brought problems, too. There were financial panics and depression when some parts of the economy got out of control. Millions of immigrants flocked to the United States from Europe and hundreds of thousands of southern Negroes migrated northward.* People were crowded together in cities that grew to twice and three times their former size.

Then, new machines began to do the work of many men and jobs became harder to find. There were violent strikes and lockouts when working men first tried to get better wages and shorter working hours. Unemployed Negroes with families to support were willing to work for very little. So, when labor unions went on strike, factory owners could hire Negroes to "break the strike." This caused bad feelings between white and Negro workers in the North.

The struggle for jobs was at the bottom of race riots like those in Springfield, Illinois, in 1904 and 1908,

* Some Americans spoke against the immigrants in much the same words that were used against the Negro. "The most dangerous and corrupting hordes of the Old World invaded us. The vice and crime which they have planted in our midst are sickening and terrifying," wrote Thomas Watson. (But the "hordes" were absorbed.)

East St. Louis in 1917, Chicago in 1919 and Detroit in 1943.

Southern businessmen were not slow to see that fear of the Negro could be used to block the organization of labor in their part of the country, and to keep wages down. Whenever it seemed that white and Negro workers might get together to demand better conditions, the old race fears could be stirred up to keep them apart.

This danger became serious when northern-based labor unions began to organize workers in southern factories. White workers knew they would be stronger if they joined. But employers warned them that the unions favored integration, that their jobs would be taken by Negroes, or that they would have to work under colored foremen. Again real issues disappeared in the smoke of race feelings. Workers usually voted against joining a union, and owners did not have to worry about demands for higher wages.

In the North, labor unions are powerful and often control the available jobs in a plant or an entire industry. For the most part, the national labor organizations have stood up for the right of all men to a job on the basis of their ability. But in practice they have often kept Negroes and immigrants out in order to protect the jobs of native-born whites. Certain large unions have barred colored members, especially in skilled trades. Only about one half of one percent of all plumbers, electricians and operating engineers are Ne-

groes. The building trades were almost closed to Negroes until a few years ago. "It is easier for a Negro to
get a university degree than a plumber's work permit,"
one newspaper reporter found.

In 1968, only 2% of U.S. doctors were Negroes; most
of these had graduated from two all-black medical
schools. Although Thurgood Marshall sits on the U.S.
Supreme Court, only 1% of American lawyers in 1970
were black—3,000 in the entire country. Medical and
law schools are recruiting black students as earnestly
as they can, but it is obviously going to take a long
time to catch up.

Big industrial firms are announcing that they will
hire Negroes in technical and executive jobs on the
same basis as whites. Usually this means that they hire
one or two for "show." But if they try to be serious
about it, they have a hard time finding Negroes with
enough training and experience to qualify.

It is still true that whites with a grade-school education earn more than black high school graduates. A
white worker with a high school diploma earns more,
on the average, than a black college graduate. Black
students know this. To them it is a strong argument for
dropping out.

It is true that few Negroes have the proper training
for skilled jobs. But they have been kept out of the
schools and out of the union apprentice programs
where they might have gotten such training. While the
shortage of skilled workers gets worse, Negroes are left
to work as janitors, freight handlers, watchmen, count-

ermen or elevator operators. Even more are still on southern farms, where machines are leaving less and less work for human hands. The whole nation takes the loss of wasted abilities.

Some opportunities come to Negroes *because* of discrimination. We have already seen how the segregation of black voters in the urban ghetto lays the foundations for political power. Something similar happens in the economic field.

A few Negroes have become wealthy in business (including over 30 millionaires), by taking advantage of the separateness of Negroes in our society. Hundreds of Negro newspapers, magazines and radio stations * depend for their success on black communities that are conscious of their separateness from whites. Negro insurance companies, funeral parlors, motels and beauty shops have been established because Negroes could not get service in places owned by whites.

If all the racial discrimination suddenly stopped, such businesses would probably suffer. Negro teachers, lawyers and doctors who have not had the best professional training might lose their jobs. Negro publications might lose readership, at least for a time. This possibility frightens some Negroes who have "made it." They may be as reluctant as any white to change their comfortable situation.

Both Negroes and whites are beginning to feel that

---

* Among the Negro press, the Chicago *Defender* and the Baltimore *Afro-American* are among the oldest and can be found in some libraries.

the costs of race separation are too high. Students at Georgia Tech made the discovery in an unusual way. Their football team had won an invitation to play in the annual Sugar Bowl game at New Orleans on New Year's Day of 1956. The opposing team was to be the University of Pittsburgh. But Pittsburgh had a reserve fullback who was a Negro. Governor Marvin Griffin of Georgia forbade Tech from playing this unsegregated game. The team would have to give up the invitation.

This was too much for the Tech students. Hundreds of them marched to the state capitol carrying signs that read, "Grow up, Griffin!" and "Griffin sits on his Brains!" Special details of police could not quiet them. Finally, an assistant to the Governor came out and shouted, "You'll play in the Sugar Bowl. Now go home!" The game was played (and Georgia Tech won).

Most of those Georgia students were not interested in racial questions or in moral questions. They were only interested in playing good football. That was worth more to them than the principle of segregation.

Their decision made them think: What is segregation really worth? Administrators and alumni of the school did some thinking, too. Six years after that Sugar Bowl game, Georgia Tech was voluntarily admitting Negro students to its classes. In the spring of 1965 a Negro sophomore was elected managing editor of the school's newspaper.

In much the same way, southern businessmen are deciding that their business is worth more than segregation. Parents are deciding that public schools, parks and libraries are worth more than segregation.

For many years, southerners have worked to make their region free itself from dependence on farming and to become a modern industrial area. They have made a good start. About one-quarter of America's industry is located in the South. The federal government is investing in dams, roads and military bases. Cities like Charlotte, Huntsville, and Houston are becoming more like the fast-moving cities of the North and West. The one big obstacle is the problem of race relations.

A growing city or state must be able to attract and keep people with ideas and the courage to carry them out: industrialists, teachers, newspapermen, lawyers. It must be able to attract and keep skilled workers and their families. But businessmen are not attracted to places where boycotts and violence interfere with business. Teachers, lawyers and journalists are not attracted to places where they cannot express their opinions.

So the best talent of the South, white and Negro, moves north; industries and professional people that might have gone to the South, go elsewhere. Professional societies and other national organizations cannot even hold their meetings in southern cities because there is almost no place where white and Negro members can be together. In business, as in politics, southerners find themselves in a corner because of the habits of race relations.

In a number of southern cities, Chambers of Commerce and other groups are trying to get out of this corner by working for racial cooperation. These "moderates" have sat down and talked with Negro leaders when public officials and even churchmen would not do so. Often they have had to keep their names a secret, to protect themselves and their businesses from threats. They may still believe in the old ways; they may call themselves segregationists. But they are businessmen first; they have looked at the price tag on segregation and found it too high.

The order to desegregate public schools was met at first by a suggestion that public schools be closed altogether. In some communities, white parents set up private schools for their children. State legislatures voted money to help support these new schools.

Again, the price of segregation went too high. Classrooms were makeshift; good teachers were hard to find; universities refused to accept the diplomas given by such schools. Many families could not afford the cost.

Little by little, parents decided it was better to have public schools with Negro and white students together than no public schools at all. Through organizations like Mississippians for Public Education and Save Our Schools (S.O.S.), they spoke out against those who were willing to destroy the public school system in order to preserve segregation.

When a federal court ruled that Negroes could not be barred from the public parks of Birmingham, city officials closed the parks. After a while, white people began to miss them. Church groups wanted their out-ings; ball teams wanted their practice fields; children missed the zoo. The officials were showered with complaints. If segregation was going to cost so much, it was not worth it. At last the parks were reopened, for the use of everyone.

In all these cases, progress came because of self-interest, not because of the law, or high ideals, or concern for the Negro. People simply discovered that Booker T. Washington had been right when he said, "You can't hold a man in a ditch without staying down there with him." It was the first step toward understanding how tightly all of us are bound in "the Negro problem."

6

COLOR AND THE LAW

LINDA CAROL BROWN was eight years old. She lived in Topeka, Kansas. Every day, Linda walked through a railroad yard to catch a bus that took her to the McKinley Elementary School 21 blocks away. There was another school only five blocks from her home, but Linda could not go there because it was for white children only. She was a Negro. The state of Kansas had a law that permitted cities to set up separate schools for Negroes and Topeka was one of the cities that had done so.

Early in 1951, Linda's father, Oliver Brown, with the help of the National Association for the Advancement of Colored People, decided to go to court and challenge the state law that kept his daughter from going to the school in her neighborhood. His case finally became the subject of one of the most important legal decisions in our history.

Lawyers for Mr. Brown argued first in a federal district court in Kansas. This court, made up of three judges, decided against him. Linda's school, the judges found, was just as good as the white school; the buildings, the course of study, the books and teachers were "substantially equal" and therefore she was not being denied an equal chance for education.

In this the judges were following an earlier decision by the Supreme Court which said that separate facilities for Negroes were legal if they were equal to those provided for other people. Linda continued to walk through the railroad yard and catch the bus to the colored school.

Oliver Brown and the NAACP decided to challenge this "separate but equal" idea. They appealed to the Supreme Court of the United States. Several other cases of the same kind—from South Carolina, Virginia and Delaware—were joined to Mr. Brown's case. Together they were given the official name of Brown *et al versus* Board of Education of Topeka *et al.* For three days in December 1953, distinguished lawyers on both sides of the case argued before the country's highest court. For five months the nine Supreme Court judges considered the arguments and wrote their decision.

On Monday, May 17, 1954, the decision was handed down and reported all over the world. The Supreme Court had reversed the ruling of the lower court and struck down the "separate but equal" doctrine. The judges had decided in favor of Oliver Brown and the other Negro parents. Separate schools, they said, are unequal even if they are just as good. They are unequal *because* they are separate. Laws that require separating children of one race from other children are improper and without force.

This decision was cheered by some people as a triumph for democracy. Other people called it a "treasonable attack" on the Constitution.

Negroes considered that May day in 1954 as the beginning of a new hope. But some people called it "Black Monday."

How can there be such complete disagreement about our highest law, the Constitution of the United States? How did Linda Brown's story become so important that it came to the highest court?

The hard thing to understand is that "the Law" is not a single, clear, never-changing thing. The legal argument between segregationists and their opponents is rarely a conflict between law on one side and lawlessness on the other. More often it is a conflict between different kinds of law, different understanding of the law and different ways of using it.

Our laws, taken all together, make a picture of the kind of society we believe in. The only trouble is that some of the things we believe run headlong into other things we believe just as strongly. For example, we have a general belief in "equality" and a general belief in "liberty." But how can we assure equality to our weaker citizens without interfering with the liberty of the stronger ones? How can the right of Negroes to have equal education be made to fit with the liberty of white parents to choose where their children shall be educated?

The Constitution seeks to "establish justice." But it also seeks to "ensure domestic tranquillity." A law that gives Negroes equal rights in Mississippi may help to establish justice, but it may upset the tranquillity of that state and even cause bloodshed. We believe in the rights of private property, but we also believe in equal treatment for all citizens. A law that forbids a restaurant owner to refuse service to Negroes assures Negroes of equal treatment, but it also interferes with the owner's right to manage his own business.

We often use the words "liberty" and "equality" together, as though they meant the same thing. In fact, they make separate claims and we must judge in each case which is more important.

It is not only in the matter of race that such problems arise, but in all public questions. Freedom of speech may collide with the need for military secrecy. The right of a citizen to carry arms may become dangerous to the public safety. Labor unions, income tax and the military draft were all at one time considered "unconstitutional" because they interfere with certain individual rights. But other concerns, of justice or of public need, led us to make them part of our law.

It is not a question of one group having rights and the other none. It is a problem of balancing the rights of one group against those of another, not so that each is made to *be* equal, but so that each has an equal opportunity to do the best that he can. Only by setting limits to the rights and liberties of all of us can this opportunity be protected. This is a problem so difficult that our wisest judges are busy at it all the time. It was this same problem that they faced in the case of Linda Brown.

The men who wrote our Constitution also tried to balance the different powers of government, limiting them each so that no one authority could ever oppress the people. The Constitution was an agreement among the original states in which they gave certain powers to a central government in order to "promote the general welfare." This government might coin money, regulate trade among the states and with foreign countries, raise an army, and so on.

In the 10th amendment to the Constitution, the states and the people kept other powers for themselves.* Some of these powers were passed on to cities and townships for the control of local matters. So, in addition to federal law, each city and state has laws of its own to deal with matters for which it is responsible: automobile traffic, marriage and divorce, the licensing of businesses, support of hospitals and other public services—and also such things as schools and voting rights that are now the subject of civil rights debate. Cities and states have their own police to enforce their laws.

* The 10th amendment to the Constitution says: The powers not delegated to the United States by the Constitution, nor prohibited by it to the states, are reserved to the states respectively, or to the people.

There has always been a difference of opinion between those who want the federal government to have all the power it needs to promote the general welfare, and those who are anxious that it have no more than it must have to regulate strictly national matters. The former interpret the Constitution loosely, in a *liberal* way. They are likely to say, "We can do it if the Constitution doesn't say we can't." The latter interpret the Constitution strictly, in a *conservative* way. They say, "We can't do it if the Constitution doesn't say we can."

In this debate, the South has usually taken a conservative view and the North a liberal view. The Civil War was largely a struggle over the right of states to tell the federal government where it must stop. And today, segregationist leaders argue that federal action in the field of civil rights is a violation of the right of states to regulate local matters.

When federal troops moved onto the campus of the University of Mississippi in 1962 to force the admission of a Negro student for the first time, they faced the Governor of the state and the state police. It was a most dramatic display of the old struggle between the federal power and the state power. In a milder way, this struggle also entered in the case of Linda Brown.

The Constitution of the United States is our highest law. Because it was written to last for a long time and to serve a large country, it had to be written in broad, general terms. Since most of it was written nearly two centuries ago, it is silent on many things that have since become important. Nothing was said about the regulation of air traffic, or railroads or radio stations, for there were none when the Constitution was first written. There is nothing in that document about political conventions, popular election of the President or many other things that have become a part of our political life. These developed later on.

The Constitution—with its first ten amendments, called the Bill of Rights—says almost nothing about Negroes. At the time it was written, most Negroes in America were enslaved. And most of the men who signed the Constitution owned Negro slaves—including George Washington, who owned more than a hundred. These men thought of their slaves as property, perhaps also as human beings, but not as citizens of the new nation. The question of their civil rights simply did not come up.

It did not arise in a serious way until the freeing of all Negro slaves after the Civil War. The 13th amendment to the Constitution (in 1865) ended slavery in the United States. The 14th (in 1868) gave to ex-slaves the full rights of citizenship.

It is the 14th amendment that is at the bottom of most arguments about civil rights today. This is the important part of it:

> No state shall make or enforce any law which shall abridge the privileges or immunities of citizens of the United States; nor shall any state deprive any person of life, liberty, or property without due process of law; nor deny to any person within its jurisdiction the equal protection of the law.

Like the rest of the Constitution, these words have a general meaning. But there is a great deal of disagreement about their exact meaning in any situation. What *are* the "privileges and immunities of citizens of the United States"? They are not listed anywhere. Are they different from those of citizens of any particular state? What is "due process of law"? If a state passes a law depriving Negroes of the right to attend certain schools, are they deprived by due process or not? What is "equal protection of the law"? Does this mean that a person in Georgia must have the same protection as any other person in Georgia, or the same protection as any person in *any* state?

Obviously, the Constitution and its amendments need to be interpreted or applied before they can have meaning for Linda Brown in Topeka. The Supreme Court exists for this purpose. But there are no fixed rules about how the Court should do its job. There are a number of tools that the Court can use.

The judges can try to find out exactly what the writers of the Constitution meant by what they said, or what they left unsaid. They can do this by reading the debates of the Constitutional Convention in Philadelphia in 1789 and the state conventions that later approved the work. They can read public speeches, debates in Congress and state legislatures. It is also possible to read the letters and papers of the men who helped to write the Constitution and its amendments. Then they can ask themselves, "What would men like Jefferson and James Madison have done if they could have considered the problem that we face now?"

A second major tool of the Court is called *precedent*. Judges refer to similar cases that have been decided in the past. Such precedents are usually very important in making judicial decisions.

There is a third possibility. That is that the Court will make a new and independent decision based on the conditions that we live in now. They may use knowledge that was unknown to the men who wrote the Constitution, or the men who interpreted it fifty or a hundred years ago.

When Oliver Brown's case came to the Supreme Court in 1953, all of these tools were tried. First the Court looked into the aged books that contained the Congressional debates on the 14th amendment. Their question was "Did the men of that Congress expect the amendment to end segregation in the schools?" They found that the subject of schools had scarcely come up at all.

They looked for the debates of the 37 states that were in the Union at that time. (Three-fourths of the states have to approve an amendment before it can become part of the Constitution.) But only Indiana and Pennsylvania had kept any record of their debates and these two did not show much conern with the question of schools.

So the judges went further. They told their clerks to find out if any state that had segregated public schools before the amendment had changed its system afterward. That would mean that they had understood the amendment as a ruling against separate schools for Negroes and whites.

The clerks pored over the records, but found little help. Several northern states that approved the amendment had nevertheless continued segregated schools: New York, New Jersey and Pennsylvania. Several others built segregated schools *after* the amendment was adopted: Indiana, Nevada, Illinois and Kansas, where Mr. Brown was now suing. Only Connecticut seemed to have felt that the 14th amendment called for an end to school segregation.

The court turned to precedent. The most important case dealing with segregation up to that time was the one that Homer Plessy, a nearly-white Negro, had brought against the state of Louisiana. He was protesting a law that required colored persons to ride in separate railroad cars. Plessy's lawyers argued that segregation by color marked him as inferior, since color had nothing to do with any reasonable aim of government. The Louisiana lawyers said that separate facilities for Negroes were not a mark of inferiority, as long as they were equal to those offered to white persons.

In Plessy *vs.* Ferguson, decided in 1898, the Supreme Court had decided against the colored man. The state, they said, had a right to distinguish between white and Negro, since nature had distinguished them by their color.

So the doctrine of "separate but equal" was born. Curiously, the only judge who disagreed was a Kentuckian, John Marshall Harlan. "Our Constitution is

color-blind," he insisted, "and neither knows nor toler-
ates classes among citizens." But southern states took
the Plessy decision as a go-ahead signal for the policy
of "Jim Crow" or segregation.

Then came the problem of interpreting the Court's
interpretation. What, after all, did "equal" mean? Did
it mean that states must spend the same amount of
money on facilities for Negroes? In regard to schools,
did it mean that courses of study must be the same,
that teachers should have the same training and receive the same pay? Did it mean that a state which refused to admit a Negro to its university could offer
"equal" education by paying his tuition in another
state?

For sixty years the Supreme Court wrestled with
cases in which questions like these came up. In general, it upheld the separate but equal doctrine, though
they often found that facilities for Negroes were *not*
equal. Southern states were confident that the law was
on their side.

But in several cases the doctrine was weakened. The
Court said, for instance, that a lawyer needs to study
in the state where he is going to practice. If there was
no Negro law school, colored students must be admitted to the white school. A student also needs to mix
with his fellow students, to exchange ideas with them.
When the University of Oklahoma admitted a Negro
named McLaurin to its Graduate School in 1950, he
was given a special seat in each classroom, a separate
table in the library and the cafeteria. The Court said

this treatment was a violation of McLaurin's right to an equal education, even though his course of study was the same as that of white students.

The meaning of "equal" had begun to change.

By 1950, many other things had changed in the United States since the Plessy decision. Education was not the luxury that it had been; it was one of the most important jobs of local government. Every state had laws requiring all children to attend school. Without at least an elementary education, one could hardly hope to earn a living, take part in democratic government, or even to serve in the army.

Social scientists had studied the Negro and his problems. Franz Boas and other anthropologists suggested that perhaps society was responsible for the Negro's position, not any physical or mental inferiority. (See page 50.) A Swedish sociologist named Gunnar Myrdal wrote a long study called *An American Dilemma;* he said equal rights for the Negro was the most important problem facing Americans, a test for our democracy. Meanwhile, thousands of Negroes were filling important jobs, becoming known as writers, educators, judges and politicians.

The meaning of "Negro" had begun to change too, a little.

The Supreme Court looked at the case of Linda Brown and the others in the light of these changes and decided to reject precedent and set out in a new direction. The direction had been pointed out in the McLaurin case and others, but this was the first time that the Court faced directly the problem of "separate but equal."

When the nine justices took their seats in the marble-columned Supreme Court building in Washington, they had all agreed on their decision. Chief Justice Earl Warren read it. These were the crucial words:

Does segregation of children in public schools solely on the basis of race . . . deprive the children of the minority group of equal educational opportunities? We believe that it does . . . *Separate educational facilities are inherently unequal.*

The uproar that followed has not died out yet.

Southerners complained that it was unfair of the Court to abandon a precedent nearly 60 years old. Relying on Plessy *vs.* Ferguson, southern states felt they had gone a long way toward providing equal schools for colored pupils, only to be told that it wouldn't do. They insisted, too, that the Court should stick to the law and not base its decision on the opinions of social scientists.

The loudest objection was that the Court had stolen the power of the states to regulate education and given it to the federal government. Almost all the southern members of Congress, in a joint statement, called the decision "treasonable." The Court had amended the Constitution, they said, not interpreted it. Some northern conservatives agreed.

The decision stands. Segregation of schools by race is a violation of the Constitution. But critics of the decision have insisted that it is "not the law" but only the opinion of nine men about the law. Ten years later, only 2% of the Negro children of the South were attending mixed schools. By 1970 the figure was still under 25%.

It is different when Congress passes a new law. This is not an opinion; it is the will of the representatives of all the citizens of the United States. For this reason, the Civil Rights Act of 1964 brought a different kind of reaction.

The Act requires, among other things, that Negroes be served on the same basis as whites in hotels and restaurants, theaters, stores and sports arenas. The federal government claims the right to make this regulation as part of its power over commerce among the states (Article 1, Section 8 of the Constitution). Opponents of the Act say this is stretching the commerce power to ridiculous size. Goods and people move so freely in our country today that almost everything is part of interstate commerce: the local café serves canned soup manufactured in another state, the hat shop on the main street sells hats made of felt from another region, the theater caters to tourists. Does this give the government the right to tell the owners of such businesses that they may not discriminate? The new Civil Rights Act does give the government that right. It has been upheld by the Supreme Court.

A few businesses in the deep South shut down rather than admit Negroes. Some owners tried to evade the law by raising their prices or turning their businesses into private clubs. But many others were glad to have a legal reason for doing what they feel is right. Most simply obey because it is the law.

Behind these quarrels over civil rights law and its interpretation there is an important difference of opinion about *how much the law can be expected to do.* Can the law change the ways in which people behave? Or is its purpose simply to record and regulate the ways in which we *do* behave? This is an old question that jurists have debated for centuries.

The majority of Americans do discriminate against Negroes. There is no question that most white people in the South still do not want to share parks, swimming areas, restaurants, movies or churches with Negroes, or to send their children to schools that Negroes attend. It is clear that many people in the North object to integrated schools and neighborhoods. These are facts, though they are not pleasant facts. The question is: can the law do anything to change these facts? Is it the business of the law to try to change them?

The liberal says "Yes! The law must lead us." The conservative says "No! The law should merely reflect the way most people think and feel."

Most people are willing to obey stop signs and speed limits because they realize that automobiles are dangerous. Most people are willing to adopt punishments for theft because they agree that it is wrong to steal. But when a law speaks against widespread habit and custom, it may be impossible to enforce. That is what happened when liquor was "prohibited" by constitutional amendment in 1919. People did not stop drinking; instead, they bought their liquor illegally. Finally the law was repealed.

The same thing will happen, segregationists say, to laws aimed at ending racial discrimination. "You cannot pass a law that will require people to like one another," they say. People will simply disobey the law and go on behaving as habit and local custom demand. If enough people do this, there cannot be enough police or federal marshals to enforce the law.

Supporters of civil rights legislation insist that this is not the question. No one seriously believes that a new law will put an end to prejudice, that it will open to the Negro all the doors that have been closed to him. The aim of the law is not "to make people love one another" but to keep people from depriving others of their rights.

No one supposed that the Constitution guaranteed that every American would be happy. It guaranteed him the free *pursuit* of happiness. The aim of civil rights legislation, say its supporters, is not to give equality itself, but equal opportunity.

Our society is built on respect for the law—even laws with which we do not agree. We have a number of ways to change the law, ways that take time and thought and public discussion. Americans, both Negro and white, are like mountain climbers on the side of a peak. The law is the rope that holds us together and keeps us from falling. We can also pull ourselves up by it.

7

COLOR AND CONSCIENCE

ONE SUMMER a teen-aged Georgia boy was sent by his church to a camp-workshop. After a few days, a Negro man arrived at the camp to be one of the speakers. The southern boy had never seen a Negro wearing anything but overalls, but this one was well-dressed and he spoke better English than the boy had ever heard before. Later he saw the camp directors shake hands with the Negro, and even eat at the same table with him. The boy from Georgia was thunderstruck.

He went off to think about it. Finally he decided that, since his church was sending him to this camp to learn something, that must mean that there was something this colored man could teach him. It was a strange idea, but the boy decided he had better listen to the guest.

The Negro spoke quietly about the facts and figures of racial discrimination. He spoke of "racial tolerance" and "equal opportunity." These ideas were new to the boy, but they seemed to be worth doing something about.

He returned to his Georgia town with enthusiasm and with scripts for a playlet on race relations. He distributed the scripts to other members of his church youth group and planned to present the play at an early meeting. The play would be followed by an open discussion of racial problems. Almost at once there was a telephone call from the assistant pastor, asking the boy to come for a talk.

In the pastor's study next day, the older man paced nervously about, talking of this and that. Finally he got to the point: the play on race relations could not be done in the church. "Why?" the boy asked. He got a too familiar answer, "Someday, when you're older, you'll understand." That was all.

The boy was shaken as he left the study. Why would the church pay his way to a summer conference, to teach him how to be a better leader, only to tell him afterward that he could not do what they had paid him to learn? Years later, the Georgia boy—now a man— remembered that day. "I remember that my heart was pounding and my mouth was dry. I felt as if I'd been caught doing something dirty."

Many young people have had an experience like this, a sudden discovery that what people say and what they do may be very different, that what is "right" may not be what is "done," and that heart and mind may disagree on what is right. In the South, this discovery is most often connected with the Negro.

A southern child who has grown up with Negro playmates, or a Negro nurse, reaches the age when it is no longer "proper" for him to show them the love and respect he has always felt for them. He learns that "all men are created equal," and then learns that he must add "except Negroes."

How is he to explain this to himself? How is anyone to explain it?

It is hard enough to discover whether segregation is useful or profitable, if it is legal, if it is based on real differences between the races. But whatever answers we find to these questions, one other question plants itself before us: Is it *right*? If the answer is "No," none of the other answers matters very much.

Most people, especially in the South, turn to their church for an answer to this final question. But the Church has not spoken in a clear voice, any more than the Law has, or Business or Labor or Government. National church organizations have made strong statements on the evil of racial discrimination. Some have recently named Negro bishops. But individual churches throughout the South, and in the North as well, bar Negroes from their congregations.

Some ministers claim that segregation was divinely established when the three sons of Noah went their separate ways after the Flood (Shem fathering the yellow race, Ham the black and Japheth the white). Others preach sermons on brotherly love but, as one minister admitted, "darn few of them are specific about who the brothers are."

Churches, after all, are run by men; and men do not shed their prejudices or their personal interests when they become priests or rabbis, ministers or deacons. If they try to do so, they may face strong opposition. The Rector of an Episcopal church in Charleston, South Carolina, was forced out of his church because he refused to agree with a decision of his board of directors to bar Negroes from communion. When a few churches in Mississippi began to admit Negroes, the state legislature threatened to tax any church that integrated.

The Catholic Archbishop of New Orleans found himself in a long and bitter fight with important parishioners when he wrote a pastoral letter in 1953 saying, ". . . let there be no further discrimination or segregation in the pews, at the Communion rail, at the confessional and in parish meetings, just as there will be no segregation in the kingdom of Heaven."

On Easter Sunday of 1963, some Negroes tried to join worship in all-white churches in Birmingham. At some they were received quietly and seated at the back. More often they were met at the door and told, "You have your own church. Why don't you go there?"

All of the people involved start from the same Bible and the same religious ideas. Yet they come to very different conclusions about how they should act—just like the lawyers who find different meanings in the Constitution.

This uncertainty goes back a long way in American history. Negroes withdrew from the regular churches and set up their own as early as 1787 because they were separated and poorly treated. Discrimination was not limited to the South. In New York City and elsewhere, some churches restricted Negroes, both slave and free, to pews in the rear marked "BM" for Black Members.

At the same time, religious feeling inspired many Americans who sought to end slavery. In 1780, Pennsylvanians passed "An Act for the Gradual Abolition of Slavery." They looked upon it as a way of giving thanks to God for the blessings they had found in the New World.

> It is not for us to enquire why in the creation of mankind, the inhabitants of the several parts of this earth were distinguished by a difference in feature or complexion. It is sufficient to know, that all are the work of an Almighty hand . . . that He, who placed them in their various situations, hath extended equally his care and protection to all, and that it becometh not us to counteract his mercies.

As slavery grew in economic importance in the nineteenth century, the moral confusion grew with it. Abolitionists insisted that slavery could not be fitted into Christian teachings. Yet there were good and pious men who owned slaves. They wanted to believe that they did no wrong in keeping human property. They were relieved when their pastors (whose salaries they paid) told them that no passage of scripture openly opposes slavery, that nowhere in the New Testament does Christ condemn it. In fact they found many Biblical passages that seemed to support the inferiority of the black man and his enslavement. Preachers especially liked that verse in *Leviticus* which commanded

Both thy bondmen and they bondmaids, which thou shalt have, shall be of the heathen that are round about you; of them shall ye buy . . . And ye shall take them as an inheritance for your children after you, to inherit them for a possession; they shall be your bondmen forever. . . .

This seemed to permit buying, selling and holding slaves, as well as leaving them to one's heirs. Paul, in his Letter to the Corinthians, wrote. "Let every man abide in the same calling wherein he was called . . . For he that is called in the Lord, being a servant, is the Lord's freeman. . . ." This seemed to say that a man ought to be content to be a slave. It was a lesson that was often preached to plantation Negroes.

A few preachers admitted that slavery was an evil, but they found reasons for doing nothing about it. It was not the duty of the church, they said, to change society. Perhaps it was not even God's purpose that all evil should be banished from this world. They urged their slave-holding parishioners to treat their slaves kindly, but assured them they did not sin by owning them.

A man's "natural rights," they said, came not from the fact that he is a man but from his place in society. The rights of a father are natural rights, but they be-

long only to fathers; the rights of property are natural,
but belong only to men of property. In the same way
the slave had natural rights, but they were not the
rights of free men.

In other words, a man's rights arise not out of his
equality with other men but out of his *difference* from
others. The Golden Rule, in this view, means not that
we should treat others as we would like to be treated,
but to treat them as we would *expect* to be treated if
we were in their social position.

These notions have held on in the South and are
now used to defend segregation. The free Negro, like
the slave, has his "place" in southern society and he is
expected to stay in it. Since his place is the lowest, he
may be the object of affection and charity, but not of
respect. He has a traditional right to cast-off clothing
and baskets of food, but not to the ballot, or a front
seat in the bus, or any job that any white man wants,
or to anything that would seem to put him on the same
level as white persons.

Most important, he is deprived of the chance to
change his social position. No matter how high a
Negro rises, he always runs the risk of being humili-
ated *because he is a Negro.*

This way of looking at human rights comes naturally
to a farming society of small towns, small business and
small talk, where custom, not law, dictates how people
should behave toward one another. Lillian Smith, the
southern novelist, recounts how the notions of the Negro's "place" seep into the lives of southern children:

I do not remember how or when, but by the time
I had learned that God is love . . . that all men
are brothers with a common Father, I also knew
that I was better than a Negro, that all black folks
have their place and must be kept in it . . . I
knew by the time I was twelve that a member of
my family would always shake hands with old
Negro friends, would speak graciously to members
of the Negro race unless they forgot their place
. . . I knew that to use the word "nigger" was un-
pardonable and no well-bred southerner was quite
so crude as to do so; nor would a well-bred southerner call a Negro "mister" or invite him into the
living room or eat with him or sit by him in public
places.

Certainly this is not race hatred. It leaves plenty of
room for good will between the races, on the white
man's terms.

The small-town southerner usually prefers to treat
people personally. He is often willing to break the
rules of segregation for someone he likes. One of the
South's most convinced segregationist governors once
refused to allot $8,000 to a Negro college because he
did not believe in education for Negroes. Not long afterward, he gave the same college $14,000 because he
had met the Negro president of the school and liked
him!

The northern city dweller may look at things differently. He may be willing to admit that every man he
passes on the street is his equal; he may respect their

rights. But he is not likely to look at them as real persons, possible friends with whom he might spend an hour in conversation. Even though racial tensions have grown in the South in recent years, southerners insist that personal relationships between Negroes and whites are more common there than in the North.

This is the curious contrast of race relations in the two regions. The northern white tells the Negro, "All right, so you're as good as I am. Prove it if you can, but stay in your part of town." The southern white says, "I don't believe for a minute that you're as good as I am, but come around to the back porch and we'll have a cool drink and talk about something else." Each thinks he is doing the best that can be done for the Negro, and calls the other a hypocrite.

The Negro has one great advantage in his fight for equal citizenship: he is sure he is right. "He has not organized for conquest or to gain spoils or to enslave those who have injured him. His goal is not to capture that which belongs to someone else. He merely wants and will have what is honorably his," said Rev. Martin Luther King. Except for a few extremists, Negroes in the movement are still determined to become full members of American society *and to make their contribution to it.* They disagree only on how to go about it.

The white community, North and South, is less sure of itself. Northerners insist that they believe firmly in equal opportunity; but how many of them, when their neighborhood or their school is integrated, complain that "Negroes are pushing too hard." A Mississippi editor can say, "We believe in segregation . . . and I mean *believe* it, like we believe in God." But he knows now that he speaks for only a few of his white neighbors. He knows that some of them are prepared to accept desegregation and a few are actively working to bring it about.

The great mass of white people are simply paralyzed. Like all Americans, they have a strong sense of "fair play." They want to reject the injustices of the past, but are afraid to make all the necessary changes. So they do nothing. Some of these are cultured, intelligent and generous people. They would be horrified at the idea that *they* are responsible for the system that binds the Negro to poverty and hopelessness. It is a comfortable system, and it includes everything that makes up their lives: churches, schools, government, professional and social clubs, good neighborhoods, the colored maid who has "been with us forever," or the Negro elevator man who has a cheery greeting every morning.

When a bomb is thrown into a Negro church, or a civil rights leader is shot in the back as he steps from his car, it is so much easier to believe that someone else is responsible—the "extremists," the "rednecks" or "white trash," even the Negroes themselves.

A white Christian layman has written that "not the extremists, but the great, white midstream of America —that is, Christian America—produces and preserves the racial chasm in American society." So the race problem becomes a "white problem" instead of a Negro problem, a problem of getting white people to understand what has been done to the Negro and how this is warping American life.

America's sore conscience is rubbed raw by people of foreign countries who point a finger at our treatment of the Negro. The United States, they say, calls itself the leader of the free world while it denies freedom to its own colored minority. News stories of race violence and police brutality are given extra large headlines in foreign newspapers, particularly in communist countries.

Our racial problem has become not only national but international, a part of the Cold War. Events in Harlem or Mississippi affect our foreign policy in Latin America and Southeast Asia. Russian and Chinese communists, who are competing with us (and with each other) for the support of the nonwhite nations of Africa and Asia, present themselves as the friends of the world's colored peoples and the United States as an "oppressor." It is not easy to explain to foreigners the history of the Negro in America and the complicated ways in which our democracy moves toward racial equality. It may not even matter to them that American Negroes, with few exceptions, have confidence that their problems can be solved in an American way.°

° The job of explaining the United States to foreign countries was given in 1963 to a Negro diplomat and journalist, Carl T. Rowan; he served as head of the United States Information Agency (U.S.I.A.) under John F. Kennedy. Later he was Ambassador to Finland.

Americans have found many different reasons for putting an end to racial discrimination: some out of generosity, some because it is good business, or smart politics, because it is the law or because it helps our foreign policy. But to people who are concerned about America's conscience, there is only one final reason: because it is *right*. They have discovered (like the boy at summer camp) that the Negro can give *us* something.

8

PROTEST

> If Mr. Lincoln could revisit this country in the
> flesh, he would be disheartened and discouraged
> . . . This government cannot exist half-slave and
> half-free any better today than it could in 1861.
>
> *First call of the NAACP*
> *Feb. 12, 1909*

NOT MANY YEARS AGO, the American Negro was the "invisible man." To some this seemed a blessing. One of them wrote, "Our greatest protection is the white man's indifference; he seldom stops to notice us, and when he does, he doesn't realize what he is looking at." But by the 1960s the Negro was not invisible any more. Far from it. Every week there were dozens of civil rights demonstrations all over the country. Hundreds of protesting Negroes and whites were arrested. Black Americans had brought their grievances into the streets—very much as other Americans had been doing ever since the Boston Tea Party.

The sit-ins, marches, boycotts and freedom rides were so constantly in the headlines that many people thought the Negro protest had begun with these things. Actually the movement has a much longer history, almost as long as the Negro's presence in America.

When black men and women leaped from the slave ships, preferring to die rather than live as slaves, they were making a very effective protest. When they ran away from the plantations and escaped into Canada, they were protesting. When, occasionally, they rose under some magnetic leader like Nat Turner, killing and burning, they were certainly protesting.

But most of these were isolated events. There was no organization and very little leadership. And there was always a strong current of opinion among Negroes that their people should accept quietly whatever white America offered to them. That at least would avoid trouble. As late as 1919, after terrible anti-Negro riots by whites in Chicago, a Negro attorney wrote:

> Some of us forget that the white man has given us freedom, the right to vote, to live on terms of equality with them, to be paid well for our work, and to receive other benefits. Now if the white man should decide that the black man has proved he is not fit to have the right to vote, that right might be taken away. We might also find it difficult to receive other favors to which we have been accustomed, and then what would happen to us?

He spoke for the very small number of Negroes who

had managed to make their way in white America by "keeping their place."

The beginning of organized black protest was directed against the movement to settle Negroes in Africa. (See pages 27–28.) The colored men who met in the conventions of the 1830s and 40s emphasized that they were Americans, not Africans. Being good Christians, they were anxious to show how much they despised the "savage" and heathen continent of their ancestors. The scorn for Africa grew so deep among American Negroes that an outstanding black historian, George W. Williams, wrote in 1883 that the African Negro was a degraded being:

> . . . his body shrivelled by disease, his intellect veiled in pagan superstitions, the noblest yearnings of his soul strangled at birth by the savage passions of a nature abandoned to sensuality—the poor Negro of Africa deserves more our pity than our contempt.

The American Negro, on the other hand, had been uplifted somewhat by slavery and Christianity. No white racist could have said it better.

The Negroes' earliest organized protest emphasized not their differences from other Americans but their similarities. Whenever a Negro could be shown to resemble a white man—in his speech, his appearance, his writing or other accomplishments—this was considered a gain for the black man's cause. The abolitionist societies of the middle 19th century sought out men like Frederick Douglass because they were pleased that a black (or nearly black) person could look and sound so much like a white man of breeding and education.

Put in these terms, it seemed obvious that Negro equality was expected to wait until Negroes as a whole *became like whites*. It was assumed that it would be a good thing if they did. That is why Booker T. Washington's famous "separate-as-the-fingers" speech in 1895 was so popular with whites and with educated Negroes. His advice was: Go slow. Work your way up to the white man's level. Then you will be entitled to whatever he is entitled to.

It is not surprising that Presidents Theodore Roosevelt and William H. Taft accepted Washington as the spokesman of his race. (Roosevelt even got into some political trouble by inviting the black leader to lunch at the White House!) But during these years the nation as a whole seemed to adopt more and more the southern view that the black man really never could "come up" to the white man's level.

The Spanish-American War of 1898 brought us new territories populated with brown- and black-skinned people: Cuba, Puerto Rico, the Philippine Islands. The old southern view of race fitted in nicely with the popular idea that Anglo-Saxon people and institutions were going to rule the world. During these years, while the Negro was directing his energies at pulling himself up, official policy and private prejudice were pushing him further into a corner of American life. Some Negroes felt that Booker Washington had "sold out" their cause.

In 1905 a group of educated Negroes met at Niagara Falls in Canada. They were angry at the way things had gone. "In its naked nastiness," they wrote, "the new American creed says: fear to let the black men even try to rise, lest they become the equals of the white." This group became known as the Niagara Movement and began to fight actively for the Negro's political rights.

The head of the group was a remarkable man named W. E. B. DuBois. He had been born in New England in a well-to-do family. He had been the first Negro to win a graduate degree at Harvard University and he had written an important book on American history. He was dry and ceremonious, wore a tiny pointed beard and carried a cane. He did not make friends easily. Yet he became the chief spokesman of American Negroes.

DuBois and his friends were convinced that Booker Washington was leading them down the wrong path. They were not satisfied with educating their people only for menial jobs and leaving them without influence on the nation's life. They put their hope in the "talented tenth" of the colored population, those men and women who had the ability to lead. They resolved to use every legal way to get the best professional training, to regain the votes they had had during Reconstruction, and to be freed from all distinctions based solely on color. They began by providing lawyers for Negroes who were trying to win their rights under federal laws.

But the Niagara Movement was without money. It was opposed by Negroes who thought it wiser to keep quiet. It had no white members who might have lent it their influence. It grew very slowly.

At just about this time, there were several terrible race riots. The worst was in 1908 in Springfield, Illinois, the town where Lincoln was born. White mobs cornered Negroes and beat them. "Lincoln may have freed you, but we'll show you where you belong!" they shouted. Sixty whites and Negroes were injured. Six thousand Negroes fled from their homes and moved to other cities.

In New York City, early the following year, a social worker named Mary White Ovington gathered some friends in her small apartment to see what could be done. They decided that the country needed a revival of the old abolitionist spirit. Out of their meeting came the National Association for the Advancement of Colored People (NAACP). Among its organizers were university professors, lawyers and ministers, writers and social scientists. There were a number of wealthy people and the editor of an important New York newspaper. All of them were white.

Many people considered the new organization too radical. Even conservative Negroes stayed away. But the members of the Niagara Movement decided to link their efforts with the new organization; and so Negroes and whites joined together to fight for equal rights as they once had for the abolition of slavery.

The NAACP began to publish a magazine devoted to racial problems, called *The Crisis*.° DuBois was its editor. "The great day is coming," he wrote in an early issue.

> We have crawled and pleaded for justice and we have been cheerfully spit upon and murdered and burned. We will not endure it forever. If we are to die, in God's name let us perish like men and not like bales of hay.

W. E. B. DuBois was the only Negro official of the new civil rights organization.

For the first time, Negroes had a powerful defender. The NAACP, working mostly in the courts, won several victories. In 1915, they carried a case to the Supreme Court and put an end to a requirement that kept most Negroes from voting in the South. Two years later another decision of the Court made it illegal to require Negroes to live in certain locations. In 1923, the Court reversed a murder conviction against a Negro because Negroes had deliberately been kept from serving on the jury that tried him. These were

° *The Crisis* is still published, and kept on file in larger libraries. Its pages are an excellent place to follow the progress of the civil rights movement.

isolated victories; the practices they condemned did not stop. But they showed that it was possible to move the machinery of American government in favor of the Negro.

The growth of cities was an important factor in the spread of social protest of all kinds. Poverty was easier to see in the city than in rural areas. New problems rose to the surface in the cities: housing, education, law enforcement, public transportation and so on. On the other hand, the cities offered more opportunities for people to organize for the purpose of doing something about these problems.

The National Urban League was founded in 1910 in order to help the many Negroes who were moving into northern cities in their search for jobs and housing. The League made the first important studies of employment, housing and education among city-dwelling Negroes. Its slogan was "Not alms but opportunity." It too was supported at first largely by white people.

Almost the only all-black organizations that could operate freely were the churches. They soon became centers of civil rights activity. Many Negro leaders today are also ministers.

After long struggle, the first Negro labor union in the country was founded in 1925: the Brotherhood of Sleeping Car Porters. This union, and its black leader, A. Philip Randolph, began to have real power among voting Negroes in the North who were members. In the South, progressive whites organized the Commis-

sion on Interracial Cooperation in order to educate the
neighbors on the evils of segregation. The Southern
Regional Council continues its work today.

The new organizations found their work hard and
slow. For most Negroes, life did not change. The federal government was more often an opponent than a
friend. President Wilson, for example, issued an order
calling for complete segregation of white and Negro
employees of the nation's government. He said that
segregation would protect the Negroes from quarrels
and criticism.

Then the first World War came. There were no
Negro officers in the Army. A training program was finally begun, but it was put under white command in a
separate camp. The first American troops to be sent to
the fighting front, however, were Negroes, men of the
369th Infantry; two of them were the first Americans to
win the French medal called the *Croix de Guerre*. Yet
French troops received orders not to be too friendly
with American Negro soldiers because it might offend
white American troops!

Under the strain of wartime, there was violence at
home. New riots occurred as the manpower shortage
brought more Negroes into jobs side by side with
whites. The Ku Klux Klan was reorganized in 1915.
Southern states wrote new Jim Crow laws. The summer of 1919, after the war in Europe had ended, was so
bloody that it is called the "Red Summer" by Negro
historians. Even Negro servicemen in uniform were
among the victims of white violence.

Lynching became more frequent than ever: there were 791 victims between 1910 and 1920. When a bill was introduced in Congress in 1919 to make lynching a federal crime, southern Senators talked it to death, claiming it was an invasion of the states' police powers. Similar bills were defeated in 1935 and 1940, despite a campaign of education by the NAACP. Only in 1959, when the last lynching was recorded, did this brutal practice disappear, due mostly to southern women who organized to protest against it.

When economic depression settled over the nation a decade after World War I, Negroes were hit hardest. They were the first to lose their jobs and their farms. Even some charitable organizations excluded Negroes from the free kitchens that were common during those hard times.

Negroes were no longer content to accept discrimination quietly. Some had fought "to make the world safe for democracy" and they expected to find democracy at home. More had migrated to the cities and come into contact with new ideas. They had gained new pride through organizations that defended their rights. Thousands more were being educated than ever before.

People began to speak of the "New Negro." And the Negro began to speak about himself, frankly, sometimes with good humor and sometimes with bitterness. In New York's Harlem district, a group of Negro writers and artists astonished the American public between the wars with their short stories, novels, articles and

poems. James Weldon Johnson, Claude McKay, Coun-
tee Cullen, Langston Hughes and many others helped
to give the Negro a voice. Richard Wright wrote about
his Mississippi childhood in *Black Boy*. His novel about
the big city slums, called *Native Son*, became a Broad-
way play.

The "Harlem Renaissance" spread to other parts of
the country. At Negro universities like Fisk and How-
ard, scholars published studies of Negro history and social problems. New Negro magazines appeared, among
them *Ebony* and *The Negro Digest*.

Non-Negro writers took an interest in Negro themes,
too. Plays like *All God's Chillun Got Wings*, *The Green
Pastures* and *Porgy and Bess* brought Negro life and
spirit to a large American public for the first time in a
serious way. Magazines began to print stories and articles showing the Negro as he is, not as his enemies or
his well-meaning friends think he is.

Negroes, at least in the North, became aware of their
political power and began to use it themselves, instead
of letting others use it. They watched the public statements and voting records of members of Congress.
They campaigned against those who did not support
their cause. In 1928, the Negro community of Chicago's South Side cast enough votes to elect Oscar De-
Priest to the U.S. Congress. He was the first Negro to
sit in that body since the turn of the century.

Economic power became another weapon in the
fight for civil rights. In St. Louis, the Urban League
began a boycott of white-owned chain stores that de-

pended on Negro customers but employed no Negroes. The idea spread. Negroes picketed uncooperative stores with signs that read, "Don't Buy Where You Can't Work"—a slogan that is still used.

During the depression years, the Communist Party of the U.S. worked very hard to win over American Negroes. For a time they even pressed a plan to set up a separate Negro republic in the South's "Black Belt"! Like many other Americans at that time, there were Negroes who were attracted to the Communist cause. But the Communists never succeeded in "taking over" the civil rights movement.

After 1932, Negroes were encouraged by the feeling that they had a friend in the White House. Franklin D. Roosevelt took special interest in the problems of Negro Americans. He consulted Negro leaders frequently and appointed many to important positions. He set up a Civil Rights section in the Department of Justice. The President's wife was just as active in the Negro cause, visiting schools and other institutions and working with the NAACP and the National Council of Negro Women. The measures that were taken to lift the economy out of the depression naturally helped the colored people, who had been among those hardest hit.

All this did not mean that there was any sudden solution of the Negroes' problems, only more confidence. The civil rights movement was still a small effort. It moved quietly and involved only a tiny minority of the Negro population. It could not be called a "revolt." But pressure was building up, like warm soda in a bottle.

The second World War gave the bottle a good shaking. Negroes were ready and anxious to contribute their share to the national defense. But even in this they faced discrimination. At war plants desperate for help, black workers faced written orders stating that they could be "considered only as janitors and in other similar capacities." The Air Force and the Marines accepted no Negroes at all; the Navy only those who would serve in the all-black messman's branch. Even the Army, in the years before Pearl Harbor, accepted only enough Negro enlistments to keep up four all-black units that had been created just after the Civil War!

In the face of this discrimination, a group led by A. Philip Randolph planned to march on Washington with the slogan, "We loyal Negro-American citizens demand the right to work and fight for our country." The threat of 50,000 demonstrators in the nation's capital moved President Franklin Roosevelt to act. He signed an order requiring an end to discrimination in factories doing government work, and setting up a Fair Employment Practices Commission.

The March on Washington of 1941, although it did not take place, showed that *direct mass action*—or even the threat of it—could make things happen. For the first time, a really large number of black Americans were organized to take action to demand their rights. Twenty-five years before the phrase "black power" became popular, Philip Randolph expressed the idea: "Only power can effect the enforcement and adoption of a given policy." The experience and the idea were to be remembered in 1963 and after.

More Negroes moved to cities to work in defense plants. Because of the shortage of housing, many black families moved into white neighborhoods. There were violent reactions in New York, Los Angeles, Mobile and Beaumont. Twenty-five Negroes and nine whites died in a 30-hour riot in Detroit in June 1943; it ended only after the President declared a state of emergency and sent 6,000 soldiers to patrol the city. Mrs. Roosevelt said publicly, "The nation cannot expect colored people to feel that the United States is worth defending if the Negro continues to be treated as he is now."

Before the war was over, almost a million Negroes served in the armed forces, about half of them overseas. For the first time, there were black pilots in the Air Force, black officers in the Navy and the Marine Corps; Negro women enlisted in the auxiliary services. There was still segregation in the camps, separate transport and entertainment facilities, discrimination in the assignment of duties and in promotions. The War Department took a stand against these practices, but could not wipe them out altogether.

World War II marked a turning point in the attitude of Negro Americans. At the war's end they were less inclined than ever to keep on waiting for equal citizenship. They had less faith in the willingness of white Americans to extend it to them and more confidence in their own ability to win it.

Postwar President Harry Truman ordered several interracial committees to prepare reports on discrimination; they put the problem clearly before the American public for the first time. As a result of one of these reports, racial barriers in the armed forces began to come down. Young men from all parts of the country shared barracks, mess tables, classrooms and showers, without regard to color. The excellent record of integrated units in the Korean war in 1950–51 proved that the "impossible" could be done.

For many Negro boys, it was the first experience of life without day-to-day discrimination. For many white boys, it was the first opportunity to know Negroes as equals. Neither of them ever forgot the experience.

In other areas, though—housing, education, employment, voting rights—Negroes were still blocked. The Congress seemed unwilling to act on the President's recommendations. Negro leaders felt strongly that some new attack on these problems was needed. No one could have guessed that it would come in quite the way that it did.

9

REVOLT

No man can tell a man who is hurting how to holler.

Jesse Jackson

SOME PEOPLE SAY it was Rosa Parks' sore feet that started the Negro revolt that lasted through the 1960s. Mrs. Parks was a small, plump woman who lived in Montgomery, Alabama and worked as a seamstress in a department store there. After a long day's work on December 1, 1955, she was glad to find a seat on the bus going home—a seat, of course, in the rear section reserved for Negroes. The bus filled up and both white and colored passengers were standing. So the driver asked the first four Negroes to get up so that white standees could sit. This was not unusual and the Negroes got to their feet.

But Mrs. Parks was very tired. She figured she was just as tired as anyone on that bus. So she said "No" to the driver. She was arrested and taken to jail.

Word of her arrest spread fast among the Negro community. Next evening, a Friday, there was a meeting of Negro leaders and they decided to boycott the buses. That meant that Negroes simply would not ride the buses; they would walk to work on Monday morning. They would keep on walking until the bus company agreed to treat them with courtesy, to let all passengers keep their seats, first come, first served, and to hire some Negro drivers on routes that served Negro neighborhoods.

At first there was no protest against segregated seating. Negroes would continue to sit from the back, whites from the front.

On Sunday morning, Negro preachers passed the word about the boycott. Women telephoned their friends. On Monday, the buses were more than half empty. Negroes shared their cars. (And a number of white people, more concerned with getting work done than with racial problems, drove their Negro employees to work.) The leaders of the boycott, headed by Rev. Martin Luther King, Jr., were indicted under an old anti-union law forbidding "conspiracy to obstruct the operation of a business." Ten months passed, and two federal court cases. The bus company nearly went bankrupt. The protesters won. Rev. King said, "We were not trying to put the bus company out of business; we were trying to put justice in business."

A similar strike was successful in Tallahassee, Florida, the following year. In other cities, where Negroes were a smaller proportion of the population, boycotts were not successful. But Rosa Parks' tired feet had started a whole new chapter in the history of the Negro in America.

There are several ways in which the "revolt" of the 1960s was very different from the protest of earlier years. First, it was no longer limited to the cities of the North but had spread to all parts of the country. Second, Negroes were no longer asking for a little more of their rights; they were demanding their full rights, right away. Third, leadership was no longer in the hands of white people and a few Negro leaders of whom they approved; black people, mostly from the new middle class, were taking a hand. Fourth, the movement had the open support of the federal government.

Many new organizations came forward after the Mongomery boycott, names that quickly became well known. The Congress of Racial Equality (CORE), born in 1942, had kept up a close relationship to the Society of Friends (Quakers). It included Negroes and whites in both the North and the South.

Rev. King's Southern Christian Leadership Conference (SCLC) was set up in 1957 and based in Atlanta. It was made up mostly of young Negro ministers and laymen who trained themselves for political action. The Student Nonviolent Coordinating Committee (SNCC or "Snick") began as the youth arm of SCLC; it had its main strength in the Negro colleges of the South.

When Rosa Parks said "No" to the bus driver, it was

nearly a century since the end of slavery. "Freedom
Now" was the motto of the new revolt, with the accent
on *now*. Instead of legal argument, the major weapon
of the 60s was "direct mass action." Teams of organizers went from one community to another when called
to help with a local protest or voter registration drive.
"We will achieve our goals by making the Negro *visi-
ble* through demonstrations," said James Farmer, national director of CORE. This meant that large numbers of Negroes—often together with whites—publicly
challenged laws that denied equal treatment to black
Americans.

Four students from a Negro technical college in
Greensboro, North Carolina, walked into a five-and-
ten-cent store one February day in 1960 and sat down
at the all-white lunch counter. When the manager told
them to leave, they refused. When he closed the
counter, they opened their school books and began to
study. A crowd of white people gathered and jeered at
them. But the students stayed until the store closed for
the day.

That was the beginning of the sit-ins. The idea
spread to all kinds of public places in many cities.
There were "kneel-ins" (in all-white churches), "wade-
ins" (at public beaches and pools) and "read-ins" (in
public libraries). Negroes picketed downtown stores
that refused to hire Negro clerks or to give Negro customers the same service as whites. "Don't buy new
clothes this spring," Negro leaders told their people.
"Wear old clothes with new dignity." Demonstrations
usually ended in arrests by local police.

In 1961 CORE began a protest against segregation in interstate bus travel. Groups of "freedom riders" boarded buses in northern cities and headed south. Students, teachers, ministers and lawyers, white and colored, they sat together, ate together and generally ignored the signs that said "White Only" and "Colored Only." Because they were traveling across state lines, they felt that federal law protected them, though they were defying local Jim Crow laws.

The first group of freedom riders was mobbed and beaten in Anniston and Birmingham, Alabama. One bus was destroyed by fire. Some riders were arrested at other stops for using segregated restaurants and rest rooms. On later rides, violence reached such a pitch that state militia was ordered out and the Department of Justice sent its marshals. But a few months after the rides began, the Interstate Commerce Commission banned segregation in interstate bus travel. Gradually the signs came down in bus terminals.

All of these protests had one thing in common: the people involved never fought back, no matter what happened. The new organizations were dedicated to the ideal of *nonviolent resistance*. This idea stretches back to Jesus and to Socrates. The Mahatma Gandhi and his followers used it effectively in the struggle for the independence of India from Great Britain. In this country, Henry Thoreau refused to pay taxes he felt were wrongly used; Quakers and other pacifists have gone to jail rather than take part in wars. Only half a century ago, American women paraded, lay down in the streets and tied themselves to lampposts in their campaign for equal rights.

Nonviolent resistance is also called *civil disobedience,* because it involves peacefully and openly disobeying certain laws. It means offering no resistance to arrest or violence. When New Orleans Negroes were trying to desegregate buses in that city, posters were tacked up in church halls, cafés and other places where black people gathered. They read:

1. Pray for guidance.
2. Be courteous and friendly.
3. Be neat and clean.
4. Avoid loud talk.
5. Do not argue.
6. Report incidents immediately.
7. Overcome evil with good.

That is one way of describing the path that the Negro revolt chose for itself in the 60s. It is not an easy path to choose. It has to be learned and practiced. It takes courage and self-control. What might happen if only one demonstrator were to lose his temper and hit back?

To prevent this, strange scenes were acted out in church basements all over the south: groups of Negroes "rehearsing" the tensions of a sit-in. Imagine it: Most of them are young, in their teens or early twenties. Some sit in a row of chairs, reading or looking straight ahead. Other Negroes walk around them, pushing them, calling them "nigger," spitting at them and knocking them down. The sitting ones grit their teeth and go on reading or looking ahead. One girl begins to cry.

Then from the back of the room an older man says, "All right. That's enough. Now you kids in the second row go up and take a seat." And the scene is acted out again.

With this brief training in the tactics of nonviolent resistance, thousands of youngsters went out to sit at all-white lunch counters, or in a library or public park that was closed to Negroes, to buy a movie ticket or register to vote. All of them went with the knowledge that they might be beaten and insulted, and probably arrested. Some carried toothbrush and soap to take with them to jail.

After a while it was even possible to find a little humor in the ordeal. Demonstrators who had spent a few days in jail returned to speak at church meetings and urge their friends to join the movement. "The food is just lovely in that jailhouse and the service is so polite," one says, showing her bruises. "I'm going back real soon and I hope you'll be there too." And on bulletin boards in Negro colleges one might see notes like "Bail Morty out by 8 o'clock. He has a class to teach!"

Those were the days of high spirits and of tremendous hopes. "We shall overcome," the demonstrators sang, arm in arm.

> We are not afraid.
> We are not afraid.
> We are not afraid today.

> Oh, deep in my heart
> I do believe
> We shall overcome, some day.

That hope could not be dashed, it seemed, by high-powered water hoses, by police dogs, by burning crosses or even shotgun blasts. How long could it last?

One man more than any other kept the movement on its nonviolent course and buoyed it with hope. He was Martin Luther King, Jr., young minister of a Negro Baptist Church in Georgia. He was a rare combination of dreamer and organizer. He was one of the leaders of the Montgomery bus boycott and a man who knew how to speak to both whites and Negroes. Like Frederick Douglass, the black abolitionist, he was handsome and eloquent. But unlike Douglass his words were always soft and conciliatory.

Three main criticisms were made of the nonviolent civil rights movement by whites and by some Negroes. One was that it brought outsiders into communities that might be struggling honestly to find a solution to their racial problems. ("Modern carpetbaggers" was a phrase often used for these civil rights workers.) Another was that all the marches and sit-ins were creating tension and making it harder for people to agree. A third was that protesters, by deciding for themselves which laws were "unjust," were encouraging a general disrespect for law.

Dr. King answered these three criticisms in a letter written from his cell in the Birmingham city jail to a group of churchmen who had called his activities "unwise and untimely." He wrote: "I am in Birmingham because injustice is here. I cannot sit idly by in Atlanta and not be concerned about what happens in Birmingham. Injustice anywhere is a threat to justice everywhere. . . . Anyone who lives inside the United States can never be considered an outsider anywhere in this country."

Negotiation was fine, said Dr. King. In fact, it was the aim of nonviolent action. The purpose of sit-ins, marches and boycotts was to dramatize the issue, "to establish such *creative tension* that a community that has consistently refused to negotiate is forced to confront the issue." Tension is not the same as violence. King emphasized over and over his opposition to violence. "But I must confess," he wrote, "that I am not afraid of the word tension."

In the street outside the Birmingham jail, Dr. King's followers sang:

> Black and white together
> We'll walk hand in hand.
> We'll walk hand in hand some day.
> Oh, deep in my heart
> I do believe
> We shall overcome, some day.

Defending disobedience to unjust laws, King quoted St. Augustine: "An unjust law is no law." The line between just and unjust laws is clear, he insisted, not just a matter of private decision. "An unjust law is a code

that a majority inflicts on a minority that is *not binding
on itself.* This is *difference* made legal. On the other
hand, a just law is a code that a majority compels a minority to follow *that it is willing to follow itself.* This is
sameness made legal."

The nonviolent Negro protest made its deepest mark
on August 23, 1963 when over 200,000 persons came
together before the Lincoln Memorial in Washington,
D.C. There had been fear that this "March on Washington" would end violently. For weeks beforehand,
there were long meetings between Negro leaders, government officials and police. The world had its eyes on
the capital to see how Americans would behave in the
face of this direct statement of the Negroes' complaint.

By bus, train and car, Negroes came from many
states. Together with about 40,000 white supporters,
they made the largest gathering ever seen in the District of Columbia. They were asking for a civil rights
bill from the Congress, for penalties against states with
anti-Negro laws, for desegregation of public schools
and government-aided housing, for a government program to train unskilled workers, raise the minimum
wage and act against job discrimination.

More than that, they were asking Americans to think
about the meaning of these problems for the whole
country. They were asking this 100 years after the
Emancipation Proclamation.

"I have a dream," the Rev. King told the dense
crowd on that hot August day:

It is a dream chiefly rooted in the American dream
. . . that one day this nation will rise up and live
out the true meaning of its creed: "We hold these
truths to be self-evident, that all men are created
equal."

I have a dream that my four little children will
one day live in a nation where they will not be
judged by the color of their skin, but by the content of their character.

John Lewis, young leader of the Student Nonviolent
Coordinating Committee, said that Negroes were
ready to march through the South to demand their
rights. "But we will march with the spirit of love and
the spirit of dignity that we have shown here today." °

The success of the March on Washington surprised
everyone, even the people who had organized it. President Kennedy said later that Americans "can properly
be proud of the demonstration that has occurred here
today." The press of foreign nations, usually very critical of American race relations, was impressed. They
saw that news stories of violence and hate could not
fully describe the race problem in the United States.

But to some Negroes, especially impatient young

° By strange coincidence, it was announced that W. E. B. Du-
Bois, the first leader of the Negro revolt, had just died in
Ghana, the African nation where he had made his home. He
had decided there was no hope for the Negro in America, gave
up his U.S. citizenship and joined the Communist Party. These
200,000 people freely gathered in the nation's capital were
proving that, in this at least, he had been wrong.

men in northern ghettos, the March was a disappointment. They felt that King and his people had taken too much advice from whites. (Four of the ten chairmen of the March were white.) They were disgusted that leaders of the March had sat down with police and other white officials to guarantee that things would go according to plan—even agreeing to close all the bars in the capital city to reduce the chances of trouble. The bitter problems of the black masses would not be solved, they said, by a "one-day integrated picnic."

Were they right? Three weeks after the peaceful March on Washington, a bomb was thrown into a Negro church in Birmingham, killing four girls aged 10 to 14. Two months earlier, a shotgun blast had killed Medgar Evers, leader of the NAACP in Mississippi, as he got out of his car in his own driveway.

The Mayor of Birmingham, it was said, wept when he heard of the bombing of the church. Evers, a veteran of World War II, was buried in Arlington National Cemetery in the presence of many members of the government. But they were all dead, just the same. And their killers were never brought to account.

Obviously nonviolence gave no personal protection to Negroes. What it gave was great moral strength to their cause. It was helping to move city, state and national government to take some action against race discrimination. The restraint of the civil rights movement impressed the nation and the world. In 1964, Martin Luther King, Jr. was awarded the Nobel Peace Prize. At 36, he was the youngest man ever to receive this international award. In his home town of Atlanta, 1500 white and Negro guests gathered in a once-segregated hotel ballroom to honor him. (A few days later, leading a voter registration march, Dr. King was arrested for the seventeenth time.)

The question kept growing: can the Negro revolt stay nonviolent? Should it? Should the black man's first concern be how whites will react? Or should it be what the black community needs?

Some Negroes, especially the older and more successful, felt that the protest had already gone too far, stirring up trouble. To others, nonviolence seemed too weak a weapon against growing white resistance.

"If a man has his foot on my neck, I tell you that leg is coming off!" is the way one Harlem boy put it to a visiting group of Negro students from Mississippi. They were not used to this kind of talk. Their only answer was: "Nonviolence takes more courage."

But how much courage was there? How much patience? How long could the discipline of nonviolence hold?

In November of 1963 President John F. Kennedy was assassinated in Dallas. His murder may or may not have been connected with his active stand on civil rights. In any case, this incredible act was like a signal that let loose all the fear and unrest that had been pent up in America for a decade or more.

In the summer of 1964 CORE and SNCC led a large-scale attempt to face down the terrorism that was holding back voter registration and other reforms in at

least one state. The Mississippi Summer Freedom Project brought over 1,000 students, lawyers, clergymen
and civil rights workers to that state. They paid their
own way and they took serious risks.

Why did they go? "I need to do something to help
the civil rights cause for my own peace of mind," a
Smith College girl wrote. "There are no more innocent
bystanders," said a Pennsylvania sophomore. "If you
stand by now and watch, you're guilty." Some white
Mississippians had other explanations. "They are all a
bunch of beatniks and commies."

The volunteers set up several dozen small schools
and community centers. They taught farm Negroes
how to read and write, and how to register to vote. Before the summer was very old, three of the volunteers
(one Negro and two whites) were shot to death in
Neshoba County. Beatings and shootings continued
throughout the summer. The news from Mississippi
helped to set off violence in the black slums of Roches-
ter, Jersey City, Chicago and Philadelphia.

Still, Martin Luther King marched at the head of his
nonviolent legions. Early in 1965, he led a "march on
the ballot boxes" in Selma and other Alabama cities.
Local officials insisted that Negroes come in twos and
threes to the courthouse if they wanted to register to
vote. Negroes insisted that this made it possible for
registrars to keep them waiting for days and to in-
vent reasons for refusing them. So they defied local
laws and marched by the hundreds to the courthouse
to dramatize their complaint. They marched by day

and with torches at night. The governor called them "mobsters" and the jails filled up. Few Negroes were registered, but the marches made headlines. President Johnson sent a strong message to Congress which led to a new law extending federal protection to black voters.

But the President's signature was hardly dry on the Voting Rights Act of 1965 when violence broke out in an unexpected place. Los Angeles was the city rated number one by the Urban League in housing, schools, jobs and other opportunities for Negroes. But on August 11 a routine arrest by a white policeman in a black neighborhood in south Los Angeles turned into a frightening six-day riot. The area known as Watts became a battleground. Snipers hidden in buildings fired at police and guardsmen. Normally law-abiding people (and some who were not) looted burning stores. Mobs threw rocks at firemen trying to put out the fires.

It was not a "race riot" in the sense that blacks were fighting whites. What black people were lashing out at was the hopelessness with which white society had surrounded their lives. That is why they were so glad to destroy "their own neighborhood." The ghetto was *not* theirs; they did not own it and they did not choose it. That is why the slogan appeared on so many walls, "Burn, baby, burn!" That is why, although very few Negroes took part in the riot and others were frightened by it, many admitted later that it gave them a sense of relief and even joy.

In the months after Watts, more riots occurred.

Ghetto rioting became a regular part of the "long hot summers" that followed. All parts of the country were affected: Milwaukee, Cleveland, Newark and Plainfield, Tampa, Omaha.

Whites who knew no more of the civil rights movement than they could learn from the news tended to have two ideas about the riots. One was that the civil rights movement itself had turned violent. The other was that Negroes were "ungrateful" for the gains already made and were "demanding too much."

The urban riots of the late 1960s were not part of the civil rights movement. They were a reaction to its failures (and as we will see, to its successes too). Watts was an area that had been pretty much ignored by civil rights organizations. People there felt left out; they had no channels through which to make their grievances felt. When Martin Luther King made his first visit there, to help "cool" the August 1965 riot, he found that many people in Watts had never heard of him. In general, ghetto-dwellers outside the South were not much affected by the civil rights acts of 1964 and 1965. Desegregation of schools and public accommodations meant little to people who hardly ever left their own black neighborhoods. Voting rights were of far less interest to them than jobs and a decent place to live.

What the civil rights acts did do was raise people's *expectations.* If the riots grew out of disappointment with the civil rights movement, they also had something to do with its successes. One lesson of Watts is this: impatience grows when people *expect* more. Now that everyone knows that segregated and substandard conditions are wrong, why should they be allowed to continue for a minute longer—especially in a country that prides itself on doing hard jobs fast? As the laws advanced, the gap between what was supposed to be and what Negroes really experienced was more obvious than before. During the impatient 60s, this same feeling drove many people to protest other issues on the streets and campuses.

But Watts remained a symbol to whites of the awful possibility of black vengeance. There was some news and a lot of rumor about black militants arming for self-defense. When Dr. King and his followers marched for open housing in Chicago, white counter-demonstrators appeared in their path, jeering and pelting them with bottles, rocks and garbage.

On April 4, 1968, Martin Luther King was shot to death by a white man in Nashville. The wave of riots that followed was worse than before. That summer there was real fear that America might collapse in interracial war. After King, what? There was no doubt any more that the civil rights movement was on a completely different course. It was a course that was puzzling and painful to many Americans, both black and white.

10

RESISTANCE

DURING 1969 runoff elections for mayor of Los Angeles, a campaign worker for Mayor Sam Yorty speaks in a tense voice to a neighborhood meeting of white voters. Many of these had voted for Yorty's opponent, Negro City Councilman Thomas Bradley, in the first balloting. Bradley was popular and had a long lead, even though Negroes make up only one-fifth of the city's population. Now there are anxious faces. The speaker hints that Bradley is "close to the Black Panthers" and other extremist groups. He warns that a victory for Bradley will mean an invitation to violence. "Will your family be safe?" he asks. Frightened by memories of Watts, thousands of voters change their minds. Mayor Yorty is re-elected.

An elderly lady sits behind a desk in a southern courthouse. Her job is to register new voters. She has seen more and more Negroes come in to register and she is worried and confused. Finally she is faced with a 19-year-old girl she has known since childhood. As the Negro takes the pen and signs her name, the woman's eyes are filled with tears. "What's the matter? Why are you doing this to us?" is all that she can say.

In the modern offices of the White Citizens' Council in Jackson, Mississippi, a pleasant young woman receptionist talks with visitors. "Our Negroes don't want any part of this so-called equality," she says. "All it means is that they will lose the help and support of their white friends here." She smiles and pins a button on the visitor's lapel; it has one word on it: NEVER.

At torchlight meetings, other segregationists inflame the crowd with fears of racial intermarriage, of Negro "blood disease," of "Negro rule" in the South and of a "Communist plot to mix the races and weaken the United States." The flag of the Confederacy is used to stir up emotions that would have shocked many of the men who fought under it. There are shouts of "Let's show the niggers" and before the night is over, crosses are burning, shots are fired into homes, people are beaten and terrorized.

Resistance to the Negro revolt is as varied as the revolt itself, and changing just as fast. Instead of being limited to the South, as it once was, it has spread throughout the country. It has adopted more peaceful tactics. It relies more on the power of state governments, as the revolt has won more support from the national government. And, just as the revolt includes many whites, so the resistance includes some Negroes.

All believe that the two races should be kept apart. For generations after the Reconstruction years, secret organizations like the Ku Klux Klan kept the Negro out of public life by force and the threat of force. The Klan was originally dedicated to "protect the weak, the innocent and defenseless from the indignities, wrongs and outrages of the lawless, the violent and the brutal" (meaning northern politicians, federal agents and freed slaves). But very soon Klan members, under the secrecy of their hoods and bizarre code names, began commiting such outrageous crimes that the organization was ordered disbanded by its own leader, outlawed in many states and denounced by Presidents.

Despite all this, various Klan organizations had four to five million members during the 1920s and became powerful enough to control state legislators and members of Congress, not to mention police departments and sheriffs' offices.

It might cost his life for a southern Negro to try to vote, to refuse to sell his cotton at the price he was offered, or to look at a white person longer than seemed necessary. So the black people of the South said "Yessuh" and "No ma'am" and kept their place. There was "no race problem," at least not that anyone could see. Senator John Stennis of Mississippi pictured the situation as white southerners saw it, in a speech he made in 1948. The southern white, he said, is the Negro's only real friend.

The white people protect the Negro and respect them in the proper and mutually understood and mutually desired relationship between the races. The southern white is the only one who really understands the southern Negro, and the real southern Negro understands only the southern white. Let them go their way in peace. Let them work out their salvation in this great section where the races live in the closest and friendliest contact and are happier together than are similar people anywhere else in the world under like conditions . . . Time is the only element needed.

Things were indeed peaceful in those days.

This make-believe peace was broken by the Supreme Court decision on school segregation in 1954. The government was no longer standing on the sidelines; it was giving active support to the cause of civil rights and to the promises of the 14th and 15th Amendments. That meant that new tactics of resistance were necessary, something more respectable than the old terrorism.

Within weeks after the Court's decision, organizations called White Citizens' Councils began to be formed in the South. They drew their membership from the "better" white people: lawyers, store-owners, editors, public officials, bankers and teachers. Their single aim was to maintain legal segregation in the South, by peaceful means. Officially, they disapproved of the Klan and its brutal tactics (though many mem-

bers of the Citizens' Councils kept up Klan membership too.) Soon the councils joined together, set up a
headquarters in Jackson and began to lead the new attack on the civil rights movement.

It is a many-pronged attack. First, the arguments for
segregation are widely circulated. The Councils publish a monthly magazine called *The Citizen* and produce radio and television programs. They distribute
pamphlets and articles containing racist arguments.
They sponsor essay contests in schools and provide
speakers for meetings of civic and patriotic clubs.

Second, the civil rights organizations are directly attacked. They are described as communistic, intent on
disrupting the country and weakening the white race.
Accusations of membership in the Communist Party
are made against civil rights leaders, both Negro and
white, even when these charges were disproved years
ago by the F.B.I. Even the National Council of
Churches (representing about two-thirds of American
Protestants) was called "communistic" for taking a
strong stand against racial discrimination.

A third prong of the attack is economic. The head of
one Alabama council explains: "The white population
in this county controls the money. We intend to make
it difficult, if not impossible, for any Negro who advo-
cates desegregation to find and hold a job, get credit,
or renew a mortgage." Negroes who register to vote
find that they are not served in stores. A Negro dentist
who became president of the local NAACP suddenly
found his automobile insurance cancelled; patients

who paid him by check were accused of contributing
to a communist organization.

With a few big-city exceptions like Atlanta, Georgia,
press and radio are controlled by segregationists, so
that there is little chance for people to hear other
views. The Louisiana Civil Rights Commission, in its
report on the 1960 school crisis in New Orleans, said:

> Seldom during this long desegregation crisis have
> Negroes had an opportunity to express publicly
> any opinion concerning the issue except in segre-
> gated Negro gatherings. None has yet had the op-
> portunity to address the powerful civic, economic
> and professional organizations.

White persons can get the same treatment. A newspaper publisher who dared to criticize the Citizens'
Councils in his city lost most of his advertisers. Ministers who offer to serve on interracial committees may
be driven from their pulpits. Lawyers who have represented Negro clients in civil rights cases have been
forced to move away. The home of the Mayor of
Natchez, Mississippi, was bombed because he had suggested that consideration be given to the Negroes'
problems. "In a way, it's harder for whites to speak out
than it is for us," says a Negro leader. "They have
more to lose!"

A fourth line of attack is the argument of "states'
rights." It is an old argument, but it has become more
important as the federal government has moved closer
to the civil rights movement. The doctrine of states'

rights is simply that the individual states—which set up the federal government in the first place—keep the power to regulate local matters. These matters have usually included education, licensing of businesses, and social relations such as marriage and divorce and the relations between the races.

This is why political speakers often refer to "the sovereign state" of Georgia, or Alabama or Louisiana. Sovereignty means the power to govern. Of course our states are not sovereign in the same way as independent nations. But ever since the Constitution was written, Americans have disagreed about just how much independence of action the states do have. Thomas Jefferson led a movement for "nullification" of certain federal laws by the state of Kentucky, laws which he felt interfered with the rights of the states and the people. The argument over whether a state might withdraw from the Union was settled only by four years of bloody civil war.

After the Supreme Court decision of 1954 (see page 77), these ideas were put forward again by some people in the South. They felt that the federal government was betraying the Constitution. There was as much talk about the danger of domination by Washington as there was about the danger of domination by the Negro. The Governor of Virginia called for "massive resistance" to the federal courts—refusal to obey decisions that went against well-established custom. Some states claimed the right to *interpose* or put themselves between the federal government and the people of the state, protecting the system of segregation from federal interference. Mississippi Governor Ross Barnett championed this doctrine of *interposition;* signs and stickers appeared saying: "Help Ross Keep Mississippi Sovereign!"

Despite the nonviolent policy of the Citizens' Councils, there were always plenty of hotheads who felt that the only good argument against equal rights for the Negro was a shotgun or a torch. The "respectable" whites said that segregation must be kept at any cost, didn't they? That seemed like permission for any kind of violence. Everyone knew that no southern jury would convict a white man for a crime against a Negro. During the few months of the Mississippi Summer Freedom Project of 1964, three civil rights workers were killed, 80 beaten, three wounded by gunfire in 35 shootings; thirty-five churches were burned, 30 homes and other buildings bombed in the state. None of these crimes was punished.

Sometimes state and federal power came face to face. In Little Rock, Arkansas, when the first schools were desegregated in 1957, Republican President Eisenhower called out the National Guard to maintain order and to protect Negro children entering school. In 1965, Democrat Lyndon Johnson called U.S. soldiers and National Guardsmen to protect vote marchers in Selma, Alabama, from Governor Wallace's threat to take "whatever measures are necessary" to keep them from marching to the state capital at Montgomery.

The states could not oppose the force behind federal

rulings. No one really wanted to fight the Civil War over again. So "interposition" collapsed. The influence of the Citizens' Councils faded and resistance took still other forms.

As the Negro revolt spread from the North into the South, so white resistance has spread from the South into the North and West. Negro population is growing rapidly in these sections and Negroes are protesting loudly against discrimination. As the walls of segregation fall in public areas like voting, eating places, hotels, libraries, parks and places of amusement, resistance grows stronger in the more personal (and more emotional) areas of housing, jobs and schools. People who are quite willing to admit that discrimination on account of race is *wrong* react with panic when it is suggested that Negroes might be their neighbors, or work alongside them, or that their children might study arithmetic and American history (let alone biology) with black children.

From the Negro's point of view, of course, these are the crucial things—especially jobs and education. It is possible, with a lifetime of training, to take the daily insults of public segregation and still go on living. But without equal access to jobs and schooling there is no hope at all.

Black comedian Dick Gregory made a wry comment on the end of segregation in public places: "I waited around for months until they desegregated the lunch counter, and then they didn't have what I wanted."

The transit bus and the lunch counter may have been where the black protest started, but it could not end there. These were only symbols of a system that pressed much harder and more secretly on black people. Black workers had much longer to wait before they could crack the wall of privilege that surrounded some labor unions and some professions. At the end of the 60s Negroes were picketing construction sites demanding jobs, and picketing colleges demanding the admission of more black students.

For a Negro family with a decent job and income, there is still longer to wait for a home anywhere outside the ghetto. Whites remain convinced that when Negro families move into a neighborhood, property values fall. Often they do fall at first. But only because so many white families panic and leave. In this they are often encouraged by real estate brokers, eager to buy up the property cheap and sell or rent it later at much higher prices.

A few people stand their ground and welcome their new neighbors. Signs go up saying "This house is *not* for sale. We believe in Democracy." Public housing is a possible solution: homes or apartments built by city, state or federal funds, and open to all. But these funds are slow in coming and white residents nearby usually vote against public projects.

In cities where there is an active program of integrating schools, white parents have banded together to protest the moving of children from one school to another for better "racial balance." They insist that they are not acting out of race prejudice; but they do not want their own children "held back" by being put with underprivileged black pupils. Some admit that Negroes have been cheated out of a proper education, but they are angry that their own children should now have to suffer for it. So they march and picket and even conduct their own sit-ins in public schools.

In short, a lot of people who had been sympathetic to the civil rights movement up to 1964–65 began after that time to feel that Negroes were "going too far." If they would just keep quiet and not complain, things would get better! There was an aching desire to climb down from the dizzy heights of moral crusading and return to "normalcy," to "law and order."

All of these unformed attitudes, mixed with the old prejudices, were called "white backlash." That was another way of saying that whites, scared and angry, were withdrawing their support.

In 1966 the Johnson administration was unable to push through a civil rights bill that touched on the delicate matter of interracial housing. Another bill dealing with equal employment opportunity was turned back in the Senate. Congressional and state elections in 1966 unseated a number of "liberals" and "moderates," replacing them with men who promised a return to "law and order."

The long, violent summers of 1967 and 1968 stiffened white resistance and frightened many Negroes as well. Politicians began to talk about a "silent majority" of law-abiding, middle-of-the-road Americans who were tired of demonstrations, frightened of violence and resentful of the pressures put on them from "extremists" on both sides. They tended to lump together all protest, peaceful or not, as criminal and dangerous —particularly when the issue of civil rights got tangled with the war in Vietnam. What they wanted more than anything was represented by the slogan, "Law and Order."

Of course law and order are not the same thing. There are only two ways of preserving both at the same time. One is by harsh enforcement: more police and stiffer penalties. The other is by seeing that laws are justly written and justly administered. The first way is certainly easier to do.

The silent majority spoke in the Presidential election of 1968. The inauguration of Richard M. Nixon signaled a temporary halt to active federal support for the civil rights movement. There was no going back, but there would be no charging forward either. President Nixon supported desegregation of schools, but he made it clear that he was not in favor of artificially balancing the races in any school. On desegregation, on voter registration, housing and other issues, he would not press any harder than the Supreme Court requires. And he filled vacancies in the highest court with men who favored a slower policy.

In many ways this is like a replay of the Hayes administration nearly a century ago. Tired from the experience of civil war and reconstruction, Americans abandoned the struggle for equal rights in 1877. For similar reasons they began to fall away from it sometime around 1967.

This is where we reach the bedrock of resistance to equal rights for the Negro or any other minority. Not in the cowardly attacks of hooded Klansmen. Not in the shaky logic of states rights. It lies in the deep desire we all have to avoid trouble, to take refuge in our prejudices and in a pinch to prefer public order to personal liberty.

11

BLACK POWER

Remember Americans, that we must and shall
be free and enlightened as you are; will you wait
until we shall, under God, obtain our liberty by
the crushing arm of power?

David Walker's Appeal, 1829

FOR 300 years the one constant fact of life for American Negroes has been their *powerlessness*. Slave or free, the black man in America has not been able freely to choose his work or the place where he will live. He has been powerless to maintain or to protect his family, or to give his children any self-respect they could keep.

He works (when work can be had) for a business owned by whites. Even in the ghetto he lives in a white-owned house and buys the products of white-owned industry in white-owned stores that hire only white clerks, white buyers, white managers. His children go to schools administered by whites and learn from white teachers and textbooks to see themselves as whites see them.

If he is in need, he resorts to white-owned pawn-shops or faces the questions of white welfare workers. His neighborhood is largely policed by whites, and if he gets in trouble with the law he is likely to face a white judge and jury, or a white jailer.

At home, he watches movies and television written, produced, directed and filmed almost entirely by whites. They show white middle-class values as the only standard—even in the growing number of programs featuring Negroes.

Those Negroes who have "made it" are in the professions—teachers, ministers, lawyers and public relations men, athletes and entertainers. They have no power to affect the economy, to set prices, to offer jobs.

In short, the Negro has no control over the conditions of his own life, except within the narrow limits set by white society. He cannot say, "This is me. This is how I am going to live." All of this is written in the present tense because, although a good deal has changed in the past few years, this basic fact has *not* changed for most black people.

All through American history there have been some Negroes who saw that what they lacked was this power to define themselves. For some (especially during slavery) this meant pure physical power, to overcome the oppressor. Others have put the emphasis on economic power, or political power, or the power that comes from a conscious feeling of cultural unity, "peoplehood," or "nationalism."

There have been a number of American Negro prophets who promised to lead their people out of bondage as the Biblical Moses led his people out of Egypt. They have insisted that the only solution to the black man's problems is voluntary separation from the white community. Some of them have spoken of a black nation, either in the American South or in Africa; others have worked for self-supporting black communities within American society.

Just after World War I, a Jamaican named Marcus Garvey named himself president of an "Empire of Africa" and urged Negroes to join him in moving back to that continent. He had at least half a million followers. Their money helped him to set up a steamship line which was to carry Negroes back to Africa. When the line failed, Garvey was tried on charges of fraud and spent four years in jail, largely through the efforts of Negroes who objected to his plans. But Garvey inspired many others with a new feeling of pride in Africa. He was strongly opposed to integration. "The NAACP," he said, "wants us all to become white. . . ."

During the worst years of the depression, a Negro who called himself Father Divine was worshipped by thousands of followers, a few of them white. His organization became enormously wealthy. During those hard times his churches—called "heavens"—attracted crowds of people with huge fried chicken suppers.

The black Muslim movement is of a different kind. It

is a religious sect, part of the faith founded by Mohammed and widespread in Africa for centuries. But the movement is political too. For the black Muslims are "black nationalists" who insist that their people, as a nation, are entitled to a territory of their own—preferably cut from those lands their enslaved ancestors helped to build in America.

The Muslims demand strict behavior from their members, many of whom are recruited in prison: they may not drink and they are rarely involved in crime or dope addiction. They are trained in self-defense and believe in answering violence with violence. They call the nonviolent techniques of other Negro groups foolish and say that integration is a trick to eliminate the black man before he becomes too powerful.

Muslims are as anxious as anyone to see a complete separation of the races. But in their view it is not the white man who is superior but the black. "There is no good in the white man," says Elijah Muhammad, the Messenger of Allah. "All the whites are the children of the devil. We must separate ourselves as far as possible, for God did not intend for the two races to mix." It is a strange echo of white racist arguments!

A splinter group of black Muslims, inspired by "Malcolm X," began to free the movement of this racist mythology. *The Autobiography of Malcolm X,* published in 1965, was the story of this man's search to define himself and to find pride in his blackness. It inspired a new generation of Negro youth, less patient and more sure of themselves than the marchers and sit-inners of the '50s. Before his book was published, Malcolm X was shot to death at a Harlem meeting, apparently by members of the rival Muslim organization. His book is still an important force among young Negroes, and one that every white person should read. °

Whether or not these organizations are taken seriously, they show how anxious the American Negro has been to find the self-respect that white people deny him. All of them have taught the Negro that he should be proud of his African inheritance—including his color—not ashamed of it. They may seem to be allied to white segregationists in their aim to keep the Negro outside of American life. But at the same time they are fighting to break the patterns that keep Negroes on the bottom of the social ladder—an aim they share with the NAACP.

The idea of black power, then, is not new in our history. But it burst on public attention in 1966, with echoes that have not yet died out.

By 1966, a dozen years had passed since the Brown decision calling for desegregation of schools. It had been two years since the great Civil Rights Act of 1964. But signs of real change were hard to find. School desegregation was moving as slowly as local officials could manage it. In 1966, about 12% of black children in the South were attending schools that could be called desegregated.

° The official black Muslim view can be found in the newspaper *Muhammad Speaks.* Published in Chicago, it has the largest circulation of all the black dailies.

Where black students were admitted, they were faced with a new kind of segregation. White students simply turned their backs. Teachers ignored black students. Proms were canceled. Black schools were closed, putting an end to proud records in sports and dramatics, and the students farmed out to white schools. Almost never were whites sent into a previously all-black school. Negro parents complained, "Our kids are not getting an education. They are just filling some seats in that school."

Those who graduated were still the last hired and first fired; they were twice as likely to be unemployed as whites with the same education. Labor unions still used elaborate apprenticeship systems to bar Negroes. Many restaurants turned into private clubs to avoid admitting Negroes. And in those riot-torn summers blacks and police more and more confronted one another as enemies.

One thing was new: an entire black generation had come of age during the years of protest. Most of them were under 20—too young to remember the days when Negroes "knew their place" and kept it. Most of them had grown up not on southern farms, nor in small towns where social controls are tight, but in big-city ghettos where Negroes are isolated and on their own. Very often they were dropouts who had taken their "degrees" in the streets.

These young people looked around them and leaped to the decision that a new strategy was needed. They were impatient with the legalism of the NAACP, with the studies of the Urban League, with the accomplishments of nonviolence. They were no longer willing to conduct their protest according to white rules, to be told "how to holler." What is more, they questioned whether the cherished goal of integration made sense. Whites did not seem any readier to accept them as equals. And blacks were not sure they wanted to be integrated into a society that seemed increasingly brutal and aggressive. This feeling grew with the assassinations of the Kennedys, of Evers, of Alabama and Mississippi civil rights workers. Most of all it grew with the Vietnam war. Young blacks asked, "Do we really want to be integrated into a burning house?"

This new generation preferred to call themselves "black" rather than Negro for at least two reasons. It emphasized their difference not only from whites but from the old Negro (or "colored") leadership. And it announced their solidarity with black people in Africa and other parts of the world who were also struggling for freedom.

To outsiders the distinction seemed silly. And plenty of Negroes objected to being called "blacks." But these young people were determined to do what their parents could not do: *define themselves.*

Early in 1966 both CORE and SNCC were split by arguments over which way to go. Should the aim be integration into American society? The policies of CORE and SNCC (like the NAACP and others) had said "Yes." These young blacks said "No." Should Negroes stick to the rule of nonviolence at all times? The existing policy said "Yes." The insurgents said "No. We will meet violence with violence."

Should (or could) blacks continue to rely on the support of white liberals? Should the movement limit itself strictly to civil rights matters and stay away from the related problems of public housing, medicine and welfare, of foreign policy and the war in southeast Asia? The old-line answer was "Yes." The new line was "No. These things cannot be separated."

The insurgents won in both these young organizations. John Lewis was replaced as Chairman of SNCC by a 24-year-old militant named Stokely Carmichael. Born in Trinidad, he had lived in New York City half of his life, gone through the fire of the civil rights movement in Alabama and come out angry. The resignation of James Farmer as executive director of CORE brought in the younger and more militant number two man, Floyd McKissick.

Carmichael, McKissick and others were convinced that only radical changes in American society would bring permanent improvement for Negroes or other minorities. To this end, they began to ally the civil rights movement with anti-war groups, with the poor, and with a variety or revolutionary organizations.

In June, 1966, the split came into the open. James Meredith, who four years earlier had been the first Negro admitted to the University of Mississippi, set off on a solitary march from Memphis, Tennessee to Jackson, Mississippi. By walking through this hostile territory, he hoped to give courage to southern Negroes who were afraid to register or to vote. He had no demands; it was to be a "march against fear." Meredith set out on Highway 51 in the company of about a dozen friends.

The next day, just ten miles into his home state, he was hit by a shotgun blast and rushed to a Memphis hospital. The news gave another jolt to Americans. It also brought together at Meredith's bedside the leaders of all the major organizations of Negro protest. They came to renew the march and to give it a clear purpose.

Roy Wilkins of the NAACP and Whitney Young, Jr. of the Urban League urged practical, limited aims that would dramatize the need for putting teeth into the Voting Rights Act of 1965. Floyd McKissick of CORE and Stokely Carmichael of "Snick" pressed for a sweeping condemnation of American government and society for failing to fulfill the promises of the civil rights acts while conducting a "racist" war in Vietnam.

Martin Luther King tried to mediate. The "Manifesto" that came out of the meeting was strong. Wilkins and Young refused to sign it. Meredith disapproved of the antiwar part. Dr. King, anxious not to create a public split, signed. But very soon after the march resumed, the difference in purpose and style was plain for everyone to see.

In Philadelphia, Mississippi, where three civil rights workers had been murdered in 1964, Dr. King said in a speech, "Anybody who is prejudiced is a slave; anybody who hates is a slave." In Greenwood, Stokely

Carmichael expressed a different feeling. "We been saying 'freedom' for six years and we ain't got nothing. What we gonna start saying now is *black power*." The language was purposely raw and the phrase hit white America harder than the shotgun blast that had knocked James Meredith to the ground. Television, newspapers and magazines echoed it across the country: "Black Power!"

But what did black power mean? Everyone had his own answer to that question. (Carmichael varied his definition according to his audience and his mood.) Did it mean aggression: "Get Whitey"? Did it mean self-defense? Against personal violence only or public police power too? Did it mean that Negroes would try to "take over"? Take over what? The whole country? The South? The northern ghettos?

Did it mean political power, economic power, or just plain gunpower?

Naturally, the news media emphasized the most sensational and frightening possibilities of black power. Millions of white Americans found it easy to believe the worst. Especially when a few small groups like the "Black Panthers" seemed to be engaged in open war with the police.°

When the confusion died down a little, it was possi-

° Even this group, originally called the "Black Panther Party for Self Defense," insists that "the nature of the panther is that he never attacks. But if anyone attacks him or backs him into a corner, the panther comes up to wipe that attacker out, absolutely, thoroughly and completely."

ble to see that "black power" was more than a cry of rage. It grew out of the convictions of the new "black" generation. These convictions are hard for whites to accept—hardest of all for those who have been most sympathetic to the civil rights movement. But we are concerned right now with black feelings, not white reactions. So we have to start by taking them raw:

America is a racist society. Racial discrimination is so deeply imbedded in all our institutions (and our hearts) that civil rights laws are not enough to create the just society we say we want.

White Americans cannot or will not make the changes necessary. Blacks (and other minorities) can count on white support only up to the point where whites feel their interests are threatened.

Therefore, nonwhites must take responsibility themselves, either 1) working for radical changes in American society or 2) withdrawing from it.

That is a hard syllogism. It all seems to follow if we accept the first statement. But that can be contradicted by a hundred examples of progress and interracial cooperation. What does it mean? That most things are owned by whites and most power held by whites? That is not news. That most people have racial prejudices that will come to the surface under pressure? That no longer surprises anyone.

What the black critics are saying is that our society has been *built* on the exploitation of nonwhite minorities (including Indians and Mexican-Americans); if this exploitation were to stop, our society could not continue to exist as we know it. Our institutions—courts, police, corporations, zoning ordinances, legislative apportionment, even public schools and welfare agencies, everything we call the "Establishment"—exist for the purpose of preserving the present state of things. Not by wicked intent necessarily, but by definition: that is what institutions are for.

Chapter 5 of this book discusses some of the ways in which racial discrimination is built into our society. Our military involvement in Southeast Asia provides another example that fits into the black power argument. Negroes have served in Vietnam and elsewhere in numbers greater than their proportion of our population. They are killed and wounded in higher proportion. This is not intended by anyone; more Negroes are drafted because fewer of them are able to get deferments for education or critical jobs. If the draft were ended and we had instead a "volunteer" army, the proportion of black servicemen would go even higher. A military career is almost the only way to prestige and security for young men who find their way blocked by racial discrimination.

The Negro suffers in our society because he is poor. In many cases he is poor *because he is black.* Sometimes he dies young because he is black.

The problem of the black man in America is tied so closely to the problem of poverty and exploitation that the two things cannot be separated. Desegregating lunch counters does not help the man without 25 ¢ for a cheese sandwich. That is why even Martin Luther

King had lifted his sights by 1967 beyond civil rights to the problems of poor people generally, and to the war in Southeast Asia.

We have a society in which superiority is guaranteed to white persons, whether they claim it or not. Most whites—even those who do not claim superiority, who are "not prejudiced"—are not willing to give up this guarantee. When it is seriously challenged (as it is by black demands for equal access to jobs, schools and housing) they will defend themselves with the institutions they control—especially the police, the most flexible instrument of all.

The nonwhite minorities cannot depend on law enforcement agencies to secure their rights or even to give personal protection. On the contrary, the police (even when they are black) are paid to maintain order, which means maintaining a situation in which whites are superior. "We are the only people who have to protect ourselves against our protection," says Carmichael.

This argument for black power versus white racism is purposely simple. It assumes that American institutions are not flexible enough to change. (That crucial question is still open, we hope.) But it is a strong argument for the ghetto-dweller who wants his life to be better *now*. It is intended to awaken blacks to the need for new tactics that do not depend on white good will.

What kind of tactics? If, as Negroes, we had to decide how to overcome the surrounding racism by our own efforts, what would we choose to do? How could we hope to win what decades of peaceful lobbying, marches and sit-ins had not been able to win—some control over our own lives?

The first reaction was to shake off the reins of nonviolence in which Martin Luther King had held the civil rights movement almost until his death. This was probably bound to happen. Self-defense organizations had appeared in black communities as early as 1959 when a maverick NAACP official in Monroe, N.C., an ex-Marine named Robert F. Williams, called on his black neighbors to meet Klan violence by arming themselves. Williams' example inspired the Deacons for Defense, a black vigilante group in northern Louisiana, and other militant organizations. (It is significant that SNCC, without changing its initials, changed its name to Student *National* Coordinating Committee in 1970.)

This did not mean that violence was adopted as a policy, except by a few small revolutionary groups that tried to imitate the guerrilla tactics of Cuban or Vietnamese communists. It did mean that some blacks at least would no longer be beaten and killed without resisting.

A second reaction was to turn from national to local issues, problems of the immediate community. This meant winning influence or control over school boards, recreation departments, poverty programs, neighborhood houses, draft boards, hospital boards. The idea was to use every kind of leverage that blacks had, to control decisions that affect their daily lives.

This could mean organizing the black vote to put

representatives of ghetto neighborhoods on public boards. It could also mean disrupting the polite meetings of church boards and welfare agencies, demanding control of funds and policy. "Operation Breadbasket" in Chicago and other cities used boycotts to force chain grocery stores to hire black workers and managers—even to stock black products and hire black contractors for janitorial services. Other groups concentrated on bringing legal aid, free clinics, tutoring, small loans, and self-defense training into the black community. This local approach came to be called "TCB" or "Taking Care of Business."

Once black people decided that what they need is more control over the decisions that affect them, they were faced with a serious problem. The black community must be organized. But how can this be done when its most ambitious and talented members leave the ghetto and don't look back, and the rest of the community live for the day when they too can forget their color? People cannot be organized on the basis of mutual shame, only of mutual confidence and pride.

The early civil rights movement had accepted the idea that white is better. Its aim was integration *into* the white society. It accepted white values as better in every way.

Young blacks no longer accept that idea. They have begun to feel pride in themselves, in their history, their talents, their strength, in their blackness itself. "Black is beautiful!"—black faces and black poise, black "soul" in poetry, food and music, and for some "Afro" dress and hair styles, and the religion of Islam. They all answer to the need that every person has for pride in one's self.

This new pride is the one permanent accomplishment of the "black power" movement. It is not a threat; it is the beginning of hope. For the first time it is possible to think about integration *with*—not into— white American society.

12

THE STRUGGLE AHEAD

Their cause must be our cause, too. It is not just Negroes, but all of us, who must overcome the crippling legacy of bigotry and injustice. *And we shall overcome.*

Lyndon B. Johnson

WHITE STUDENTS WHO enroll in courses in black history usually express the feeling that they ought to know more about the Negro and "his problems." After a month or two a few begin to suspect that this is not the real point. The "Negro problem" exists because white Americans created it. It continues to exist because we are confused about who and what *we* are.

There are two ways of looking at America. The familiar one is this:

America is a nation founded by white people, mostly of Anglo-Saxon descent, seeking personal liberty in a new land. After they founded the earliest colonies in

Virginia and Massachusetts, other people joined them: Germans, Irish, Negroes; later on Italians, Poles, Russians, Mexicans, Chinese and so on. These people gradually accepted the way of life of the "native" Americans, and were mostly accepted into it. Thus America became a "melting-pot" where people of all kinds merged into a uniquely free, English-speaking people, with a democratic form of government inherited from the English common law and elaborated on the frontier. America was defined by its founders. But anyone can become an American if he wants to, by learning English and adopting American ways.

This is an attractive picture and it is roughly the way Americans learned about their country for 200 years. But it raises some thorny problems.

First of all, it is not strictly true. There were Irish Catholics, Germans, Jews, Frenchmen—and Negroes—in the earliest North American settlements: Danes in Delaware, Dutch in New York, Germans in Pennsylvania. As early as these, the Spaniards were exploring and settling Florida and the Southwest, the French in Louisiana and east Texas. In 1776, when the Declaration of Independence was adopted, Spanish missionaries were founding what is now San Francisco, California; San Antonio, Texas, was a Spanish-Indian settlement over half a century old.

We usually think of this country as beginning on the eastern seaboard and growing slowly westward. In another sense, though, it was established at the edges and grew toward the middle.

There is a more serious problem with the traditional view of America. If America is by definition what the early colonists established, then all the changes that have happened since then—the arrival of Negroes, Catholics, Jews, the encounter with the Indian, with Frenchman, Spaniard and Mexican—are more or less unfortunate accidents. Something has to be done to correct these accidents so that the "real" America will survive. Either the strangers must change, or be put in a subordinate position to the "real" Americans. The melting-pot must not have lumps in it. Black lumps are the easiest to spot.

The Negro "accident" was solved first by slavery, then by segregation and exploitation. Since Negroes were "obviously" not like other Americans and could never be assimilated (except by intermarriage on a large scale), they were set apart as a kind of colonial possession in our midst. They, like other minorities, were not "us," not quite Americans. From this point of view, a generous attitude was to try to understand them, to lessen their hardship and to help them become as much a part of American society as might be possible for them. Many generous people sincerely hold this view—including those students we mentioned at the beginning of the chapter.

But there is another way of looking at America:

America has not been finally defined, not in 1620, nor 1776, nor at any other moment in time. Every group that comes to America helps to define it; this, in fact, is its only definition. America is, in its deepest

being (not merely in numbers) part Negro, just as it is
part Scotch-Irish, part Spanish, part Indian, or Greek.
This nation is less a melting-pot than it is a welding-
shop. The parts do not disappear in the whole; they
make *it, changing its shape with each new addition.*
America is what it becomes. Anyone can become an
American if he wants to, by being here and making his
own contribution *to the definition.*

America, in this view, is always unfinished, always
remaking itself. It is a "pluralistic" society in which different life-styles, beliefs, traditions and speech can exist
side by side and profit from one another.

If we accept this view, the problem is no longer to
understand the outsider, to "make allowances" for him,
or to help him become like us. We have only to *accept*
him, because as he is, he is already part of ourselves.
As Pogo would say, "They is us."

For the student in that black history course the
problem is now to understand himself, to discover as a
white American how black he is, how black is America.
So we come to the question of our own identity, a
question that black writers like James Baldwin have already titled (with a bit of wry humor) the "white problem."

Try to imagine what America would be like without
blacks. Would it be better? Our Revolution would
have been a different kind of experience and the Constitution a different document. The moral anguish of
the years before the Civil War would be missing—and

with it half of our literature. Possibly the war itself
would not have occurred, with its tremendous results.
Our music, our speech and our humor, our sports, our
food would not be what they are.

This is what begins to come through (or should) in
the study of "black history." America is not a white
country where black people happen to live. America is
part black.

Understanding this is our first job. From this understanding comes acceptance of ourselves and of one another. Not tolerance; acceptance. Not acceptance
based on others' ability to become like us; acceptance
of others as they are, and for what they may have to
contribute out of their own being.

Now it becomes clearer just how much we have
done and how much we have left to do. In the past
decade or so, Americans have nearly accomplished the
job of legal desegregation. But desegregation is a nega-
tive action: the lowering of legal and customary barriers that keep Negroes from the basic rights of voting,
education and personal dignity. That brings us up to
where we should have been in the first place.

Integration is a much longer step and one that is less
clearly defined. It has to be defined starting now, by
blacks and whites together; and integration defined by
one for the other would only be the re-establishment of
racial barriers in new positions. The job of the 1970s is
to secure the widest possible participation of black

people (and other minorities) in all kinds of activities, on the same basis as whites. This cannot be done by passing laws. It has to be worked out together and it may work differently in different times and places. Participation may be separate in some cases, together in others; what matters is that the decision be a free one on both sides.

Some people feel that in order for the Negro to overcome the special problems left by so many years of discrimination he needs active help for a time. Some black leaders are arguing for special action by government, churches and other institutions, to make up for the handicaps placed on them in the past. Some call this "reparations": funds to help black communities and businesses, special consideration to Negro applicants for universities, for skilled jobs and positions in government. They insist that Negro and white school children be shifted if necessary to create interracial schools. Sometimes the demands are symbolic, as when black students at the University of Texas at Arlington persuaded the student body to change the name of their athletic teams from "Rebels" to "Mavericks."

Many people are opposed to this kind of special treatment. It is a kind of discrimination in reverse. Those who favor the idea point out that black Americans have been getting special treatment of the wrong kind for 200 years or so. Also, the government gives special attention to other groups with special problems (the farmer, for example), and to underdeveloped foreign countries. Why not offer such help temporarily to our own people who may need it? "They" is "us."

Deep down, many white people feel that all this is a favor to the Negro, and something for which whites must pay. In the long run it should be just the opposite. Acceptance and integration will mean that Negroes can contribute, on the same basis as others, to the direction this country takes. That is what most Negroes seem to want. "For years we've just been trying to get on the train," one black writer has said. "No one has thought to ask where the train is going." In the past few years, more have been asking; as a result, more whites have been asking. That is as it should be.

It is wrong to suppose that equality can be given. By definition, what is given can be taken away again.

It is wrong to think that equality can be seized by force. What is seized can be seized back by superior force.

Equality can only be acknowledged.

Both Negroes and whites are going to have trouble getting used to a new relationship. "For a long time we could justly blame the white man for our weaknesses and shortcomings," says Negro writer Louis Lomax. "This day is about over." The white man, for his part, will have to stop using the Negro to make himself feel superior.

This kind of change is not easy to make. People on both sides are discouraged to see that the struggle over civil rights has seemed to make relations between the races worse instead of better. Perhaps there are fewer friendships between Negroes and whites in the South today than there were fifteen or twenty years ago. Conversations on the street, in the kitchen or the feed store are not long and relaxed as they used to be. Students at white colleges who used to visit a nearby Negro college for a concert or lecture do not go any more, or they go secretly. In the North, people who have always thought they had no prejudice are now angry because Negroes are "making trouble."

Perhaps it has all been a mistake, some people say. Perhaps things really were better in the "good old days."

But people in the civil rights movement do not worry much about these new tensions. Some tension is necessary if things are to move ahead, they say. The opposite of tension, after all, is relaxation. A high-jumper must have his muscles tensed if he wants to clear the bar; if they are relaxed, he will never get off the ground.

Civil rights leaders admit that they want to create tension—not violence, but "useful tension." They want Americans to stop relaxing in their comfortable habits of discrimination and start exercising their principles. They want to force all of us to accept the fact of equal rights for all Americans. Frederick Douglass said, "If there is no struggle, there is no progress. Those who profess to favor freedom, and yet deprecate agitation are men who want crops without plowing up the ground. They want the ocean without the awful roar of its many waters."

If this means that the old relationship between the races must be destroyed, most Negroes will not regret it. Too many of the old friendships were based on the white man's feeling of guilt and the Negro's fear or his need of help. Once the law has established the rights of all citizens, the Negro and the white will have to stand on their own merits. Then they can begin to know one another.

In many other countries, there is racial discrimination but the tensions are hidden. In some African nations where a white minority rules, colored persons are treated like conquered subjects and forced to live in separate communities. In some Latin American countries, native Indians are barred from public places. In the Negro nation of Haiti, blacks discriminate against mulattos. There is discrimination against Asian nationalities in the Soviet Union. In some of these countries there is "less tension" because there is less freedom to protest; in some because there is less to hope for.

The Swedish observer Gunnar Myrdal, when he returned to the United States in 1970, was astonished at the changes in race relations. Americans were scarcely aware of how much they had done, he said, especially in the South. There is bitterness and frustration, of course. But there is also the certain knowledge that things can be changed. Negroes in the United States know that a better life is possible; they have proved that our democratic system offers them a way to share in it That is *why* there is impatience and tension and agitation. (There will be more of it as Negroes get closer to their goal, not less.) That is why there is still hope that the United States may become the world's first truly interracial society.

OTHER BOOKS TO READ

Baldwin, James, THE FIRE NEXT TIME. Dial Press 1963. Strong personal statement by a black writer.

Bardolph, Richard, THE NEGRO VANGUARD. Random House 1959. Study of 131 Negro leaders since the American Revolution.

Bontemps, Arna and Conroy, Jack, ANYPLACE BUT HERE. Hill & Wang 1967. Concentrates on city problems: Detroit, Chicago, Watts.

Botkin, B. A., editor, LAY MY BURDEN DOWN: A Folk History of Slavery. University of Chicago 1945. Told by ex-slaves.

Carmichael, Stokely and Hamilton, Charles, BLACK POWER: THE POLITICS OF LIBERATION IN AMERICA. Random House 1967.

Chu, Daniel and Skinner, Elliott, A GLORIOUS AGE IN AFRICA. Doubleday 1965. The African past we know so little about.

Duberman, Martin, IN WHITE AMERICA. New American Library (Signet) 1965. A two-act dramatic reading depicting the history of the Negro in the United States, from actual documents.

Franklin, John Hope, FROM SLAVERY TO FREEDOM, A History of Negro Americans. Random House 1967 (3rd edition). One of the best one-volume histories.

King, Martin Luther, Jr., WHERE DO WE GO FROM HERE: CHAOS OR COMMUNITY? Bantam Books 1967. Dr. King's last book.

Muse, Benjamin, THE AMERICAN NEGRO REVOLUTION, From Nonviolence to Black Power 1963–1967. Indiana University Press 1968.

Smith, Lillian, KILLERS OF THE DREAM. W. W. Norton 1961 (revised). A southern white speaks against racial injustice.

Wright, Richard, BLACK BOY. Harper 1945. One of the most influential American Negro writers, on growing up black.

X, Malcolm and Haley, Alex, THE AUTOBIOGRAPHY OF MALCOLM X. Grove Press 1965.

INDEX

THE AUTHOR

David Bowen grew up in Chicago and New York City and graduated with honors from Harvard in 1951. Although he had been interested in writing from the age of nine, he entered the theater after graduation, and was a producer of a successful off-Broadway venture. Later he received a Master's degree in history from the City College of New York. He has been a teacher of history at St. Mary's University in San Antonio, Texas.

Mr. Bowen has had a keen interest in the race problem in the United States since he lived in Raleigh, North Carolina in the mid-1950s. During the spring of 1963, at the time when Birmingham erupted, Mr. Bowen traveled throughout Louisiana, Mississippi, Alabama and Georgia, and, in 1964, he traveled through Texas and Tennessee. On each trip he observed demonstrations and interviewed leaders and demonstrators on both sides.

David Bowen has also lived in Latin America, and

he is the author of *Hello, South America, Hello, Brazil,* and other books. He has contributed articles to the *Book of Knowledge, The Reporter, The New York Times* and the *National Observer.* He lives in San Antonio.